AND NOW FOR THE BBC ...

This book is to be ret... ...nd University of Manchester

Broadcasting Symposium

X

302.23
AND.
src

Editors:

Nod Miller
University of Manchester School of Education
(Symposium Director)

Rod Allen
Chief executive, Television Entertainment, London

Published with the support of Thames Television plc

AND NOW FOR THE BBC ...

Proceedings of the 22nd University of Manchester

Broadcasting Symposium

Edited by

Nod Miller

University of Manchester School of Education

Rod Allen

Television Entertainment

Current Debates in Broadcasting: 1

John Libbey

JL

LONDON · PARIS · ROME

British Library Cataloguing in Publication Data

Miller, Nod
    And now for the BBC ...
    Current Debates in Broadcasting: 1
    I. Title II. Allen, Rod III. Series

ISBN: 0 86196 318 0

ISSN: 0963-6544

Published by
John Libbey & Company Ltd, 13 Smiths Yard, Summerley Street, London
SW18 4HR, England.
Telephone: 081-947 2777: Fax 081-947 2664
John Libbey Eurotext Ltd, 6 rue Blanche, 92120 Montrouge, France.
John Libbey - C.I.C. s.r.l., via Lazzaro Spallanzani 11, 00161 Rome, Italy

Contents

Sponsors

The Symposium Steering Committee would like gratefully to acknowledge the Symposium's supporting bodies:

BBC
Independent Television Commission

ITV Association
Channel 4 Television Company

and its generous sponsors:

Action Time
BBC North
BECTU
Granada Television
Granada Studio Tours

National Transcommunications
Television Entertainment
Thames Television
TV-am

In organising the Broadcasting Symposium, the School of Education of the University of Manchester is advised by a Steering Committee whose members are:

John Gray, independent consultant (chair)
Nod Miller, University of Manchester (director)
Marjorie Burton, University of Manchester (administrator)

Roy Addison, Thames Television
Rod Allen, Television Entertainment
Lesley Aston, Independent Television Commission
Steven Barnett, Henley Centre
Andrew Curry, independent producer
Sue Elliott, Independent Television Commission
Lynne Fredlund, independent producer
Paul Habbeshon, BBC
Jocelyn Hay, Voice of the Listener
Jerry Kuehl, Open Media

Ian Lindsley, BECTU
Mary McAnally, Thames Television
Robin McCron, BBC
Graham Murdock, University of Loughborough
Cresta Norris, TV-am
Clare Reynolds, Broadcasting Standards Council
Colin Shaw, Broadcasting Standards Council
Brook Sinclair, independent consultant
Charles Tremayne, Granada Television

Transcriptions by Francesca Garcia-Quismondo and Alltypes Business Services

Introduction

Nod Miller
Lecturer in Adult Education and Mass Media, School of Education,
University of Manchester
Symposium Director

In 1996, the government must renew the BBC's Charter and Licence – the statutory instruments under which the BBC operates as a public service broadcasting organization. In the 1980s, the broadcasting debate focused on the deregulation of the commercial sector, culminating in the far-reaching 1990 Broadcasting Act and the new-style ITV licence renewals in 1991. Having disposed of the commercial sector in a radical manner, the government is now expected to turn its attention to the BBC with equal disregard for the status quo. One could almost imagine the mandarins at the Home Office rubbing their hands and muttering "And now for the BBC ..."

It was this image which prompted the Steering Committee of the University of Manchester Broadcasting Symposium to settle on the future of the BBC as the topic for the 1991 gathering, with the hope that it might be possible to identify some of the agenda items for the coming debate.

As usual, the Symposium attracted participants who were able to bring a wide range of perspectives to bear on the issues. They included policy- and programme-makers, administrators, regulators, trades unionists, journalists, consultants, academics and students. A number of overseas participants contributed experience of alternative models of public service broadcasting.

This book contains the Proceedings of the 1991 Symposium. While some of the text is taken from papers prepared in advance and read in Manchester, most of the material is made up of edited versions of extemporised speeches and spontaneous discussion, recorded on tape and transcribed. In editing this material we have tried to retain the language and flavour of lively interchange which characterized the Symposium. We feel that the content of our discussion will prove of lasting interest to all concerned with the future of public service broadcasting.

Anthony Smith, who has been at the centre of debates on broadcasting policy since he published his radical proposals for the fourth television channel over twenty years ago, reflects with some gloom on the recent history of public service broadcasting in his keynote speech. He argues that the changes which have been wrought to date in the public service broadcasting environment have been driven by the Thatcherite

1

ideology of market competition; he expresses anxiety that this thinking will be extended to inform the remoulding of the BBC. He asserts that the BBC must guard against being forced into a marginal position whereby it becomes merely a repository for programmes which commercial interests are not prepared to support.

Anthony Smith's account of what happens when "Broadcasting Meets the Social Market" is followed by a series of panel discussions focusing on particular dimensions of the debate about the future of the BBC. The first of these explores some implications of possible changes for programme-makers, both inside and outside the BBC. Contributors to the second panel debate the pros and cons of funding the BBC through advertising.

New ground for the Symposium is broken in a session which deals with engineering issues; contributors here demonstrate the interplay of technology and politics, and reveal the extent to which political demands from Brussels are likely to overshadow those from Westminster in shaping engineering developments in the future.

A further three panellists address the question of whether we are about to see "The End of BBC Radio As We Know It", and attempt to predict the shape of radio services in a competitive future. The debate here parallels that in television, with the importance of retaining commercial-free popular programming as well as a service for minority interests being defended stoutly; arguments for keeping Radio 1 free from advertising are made as strongly as those for the preservation of a commercial-free Radio 4.

Two further sets of presentations examine the direct interface between broadcasters and politicians. In a debate dealing with the television coverage of the recent conflict in the Middle East, an academic researcher, an MP and two senior broadcasters who contributed to the tone of television news coverage advance conflicting views on the contention that the BBC acted as "The Baghdad Broadcasting Corporation" during the Gulf War. This session was added to the Symposium programme at a late stage in the planning of the event. Members of the Steering Committee felt that the issue of how broadcasters deal with war was too important to be overlooked.

The relationship between broadcasters and politicians is at the heart of the debate about the future of the BBC, and the significance of the political interview, as the most visible manifestation of this relationship, is dissected by contributors to a session entitled "I'm Glad You Asked Me That ...".

Four further contributions complete this volume. My co-editor Rod Allen provides a sketch of the "Parliamentary" debate on a fictitious Bill to break up the BBC which was staged in the Granada Studio Tours House of Commons set. He suggests that a central theme of this debate is the failure of the BBC to pay sufficient heed to the demands of its closest friends for accountability and access.

In recent years, a participative group exercise has been established as one of the distinctive features of the Manchester Symposium. Andrew Curry was responsible for devising an ingenious scenario for the 1991 simulation exercise, which enabled participants to experience directly some of the pressures faced by the BBC management; he describes what happened when competing teams were presented with the challenge: "It's Your BBC: Now Run It". At the end of his account, he draws attention to some real-life lessons to be derived from the behaviour of the groups in this exercise. The close parallels between the microcosmic realities of simulation exercises and their real world counterparts were highlighted for me on 15 May 1991 when television news viewers were treated to the spectacle of representatives of ITV companies and their competitors arriving at the ITC headquarters to deposit their franchise applications and sealed envelopes containing bid prices. This process was strongly reminiscent of Symposium simulation exercises we have staged in past years – although the scenario of a blind auction for television franchises would no doubt have been dismissed as unbelievable only three or four years ago.

Jim Brown, a Symposium participant who was one of the architects of a successful plan to turn the BBC into a workers' co-operative during this year's simulation, offers his interpretation of the event, and some provocative thoughts on public service broadcasting policy.

Finally, Steven Barnett, Head of Media Futures at the Henley Centre for Economic Forecasting and a member of the Symposium Steering Committee, gives an overview of the policy issues debated during the Symposium and explores possible directions in which the BBC may go – or be pushed. He gives an analysis of policy recommendations offered in recent reports from think-tanks ranged across the political spectrum, and returns to some of the questions raised in Anthony Smith's opening presentation.

The 1991 Symposium was the 22nd such gathering. The event has a self-renewing quality, in that each year a loyal core of regular participants is joined by a healthy proportion of newcomers, many of whom go on to join the regulars in subsequent years. I believe that participants engage readily with the culture of the event, which is difficult to convey between soft covers.

We hope that the debates published here will entertain as well as inform and educate, but readers of this text will miss out on some of the jokes, the fun and the prizes of the lived experience. You have to attend to find out about the ingenious learning event provided in Action Time's game show *Top Table*, or the dirt dished on participants by Mr Manchester, gossip columnist of the Symposium newspaper, the *Manchester Daily Beast*. I hope that readers who are not Symposium regulars will be sufficiently intrigued to join the Symposium in future years.

1 Keynote: Public service broadcasting meets the social market

Anthony Smith
President, Magdalen College, Oxford

Chair: Professor Peter Mittler
School of Education, University of Manchester

Professor Peter Mittler: We are very pleased indeed that this 22nd Symposium is being held here. It's a long tradition. It was about the time when I first came to this University that these conferences began, and the University and the School of Education are really delighted that we are able to continue to host this Symposium. I hope we'll be doing so for a very long time indeed.

I understand that the Symposium is very well known in broadcasting circles and one of its distinguishing features obviously is that it brings together, in a friendly and informal atmosphere, both broadcasters and academics. I think the residential element of the conference is one key factor in its success.

Speaking for the School of Education, we are particularly delighted that we have an M.Ed. in Education and the Mass Media and that Dr Nod Miller, who is directing this Symposium, is directing that programme. I can tell you it is a very successful programme indeed; it is an innovative course. We have a lot of takers for it; it's one of the healthiest parts of our Master's Degree programme.

I am also particularly delighted to welcome our speaker, Anthony Smith, who is President of Magdalen College, Oxford. I am delighted to welcome him for many reasons not the least of which is that he combines in one person the careers of both broadcasting and academia. So I welcome him as a fellow academic just as professional broadcasters here will welcome him as a colleague and as a leader. Anthony Smith has a long record in television and in broadcasting and many of you will know him as producer of BBC current affairs programmes over a long period, particularly *Twenty Four Hours*. It's a programme I certainly remember well; I go back a bit as a viewer. He was also a member of the somewhat controversial Annan Committee on the Future of Broadcasting. Having sat at Lord Annan's feet when I was an under-

4

graduate student at Cambridge, I just wonder how much he's changed. Every time I hear him, or listen to him, I don't think he has changed at all from the time when he taught history at King's College, Cambridge; he has that same brilliant capacity to take an overview of complex developments.

Anthony Smith has also been the Director of the British Film Institute and a Director of the Channel 4 Television Company for a number of years. And now, most recently, he has taken on what is probably one of the most onerous and difficult and controversial jobs. He offered himself up as a hostage to fortune as a member of the Arts Council of Great Britain.

So he comes to you, this afternoon, to give this keynote address in the middle of a distinguished and very productive career.

Anthony Smith: When we talk about and often even when we practise the crafts of broadcasting we use the words "public" and "private," "commercial" and "independent" as if they are definitions of separate and autonomous sectors of the two media. In fact these terms are but the shards of old political debates, the frayed rags and chewed bones of old doctrines which have become embedded in the language which encases these cultural institutions. As the years pass they have come to have overlapping meanings and as new policy debates arise they become often the convenient means of obfuscation; listen to any internal industry discussion and you can hear how these words hang around like redundant metaphors waiting for something to signify, unemployable words insisting on secure work in out-of-date institutional machinery.

These and many other terms, however, are used to organize our thinking about the two media of radio and television. The issue, which has always been crucial, as to whether these media are public or private, independent or commercial, was thrown up by a dilemma, which goes back to the very technical and political origins of broadcasting; the issue was whether to treat radio and television as industries which provide the materials of a modern culture or instead as a set of cultural activities which pass through society via the apparatus of two industries. Which comes first? And why?

In the 1920s it was the wireless set manufacturing industry which asked government to set up a special company to send out material to the new audience and so encourage people to buy receiving equipment. The industry of manufacture left it to the new public body – which was posed often uncomfortably and sometimes even perilously in that vacant space between the governmental and the private/industrial – to deal with the difficult problems associated with the music and newspaper industries, theatre and, later, cinema – with all the software in fact. Both dimensions of broadcasting have of course remained on the agenda of government, and the official administrative framework which has evolved from decade to decade is still concerned with both supervising the content and finding the right organizational framework.

Governments have from the start been notoriously highly sensitive to the content of broadcasting. Whatever solutions were offered from time to time the basic decision of who was to use the spectrum and whether for personal or other benefit remained with government. No government has ever shed the responsibility however hard they have tried to re-label the problem. Even where a society has tried to reduce governmental involvement to the merest and most technical fragment, it has eventually found itself building a complex and often rather invasive apparatus of supervision.

These concerns of government have never been allayed; however the two media have matured. Unlike any other industry or art form, radio and television have never evolved any internationally accepted or even intra-nationally accepted organizational form. Every change in technology was used as the argument or excuse for a fresh look at the institutions and professional practices and the sources of revenue. Britain, with what are surely two of the world's most stable broadcasting institutions, has had no fewer than seven major public commissions of enquiry since the 1920s. France has passed through four dramatically different stages. The United States has almost never been without its courts and several governmental agencies being in the midst of quite serious rule-making and rule re-making.

In the last decade, and still today, attention is again being paid, right across the OECD countries and now in the re-emerging societies of central Europe, to the questions of how to reorganize radio and television with the intention, in many cases, of enabling commercial enterprises to enter into fields previously occupied by public interest bodies. The content of radio and television as well as the ownership of radio and television distribution systems (which have themselves become diverse) have today both become the material of extremely large and strategically important international businesses. They are likely to become even bigger between now and the end of the century. New means of distributing moving images through cable and satellite are being brought into commercial use and have to be provided with institutional housing. In Britain we have now settled some of these issues for a time at least, but, for reasons which I shall try to set out, we are on the brink of a further major discussion – around the future of the BBC – which could have the effect of altering the entire mechanism all over again in the latter part of the present decade.

I think the BBC should go on, as it is, with the licence fee as its main support; I think it ought to exist not as a marginalized and carped-at survival of an earlier era of broadcasting but as the central instrument of the broadcast culture, as the largest continuing source of programmes, programmes which could find their way into all parts of the system which has now, for better or worse, been established. I think the BBC should proclaim its purpose and not apologize for it. I think those concerned about the state not only of the television medium, but of the state of mind of the country, should start the process of explaining to government how necessary this institution is. My argument is about the BBC, but it will take a somewhat circuitous route.

In the 1980s this country became embroiled in the issue of deregulation, a term which had become used in the United States, more frequently by liberals than by conservatives, to describe the policy of making companies compete more vigorously in the interests of the consumer. To deregulate meant to remove the props of government and to sweep away irksome official interference. The end result was to make industries stronger through competition and to force companies to pass the benefit to the consumer through improved service and lower prices. The United States has had long experience in handling industries which are virtual monopolies and are therefore subjected to a high degree of supervision by government agencies. Such companies become greedy – so it is believed – and less technologically dynamic; the removal or alteration of government controls and the elimination by slices of areas of monopoly help pricing to become sharper and increases the willingness to innovate. Deregulation, however, does not lead to companies becoming free of all rules. Far from it. New systems of regulation have to take the place of the old ones to ensure that the new competitive position continues and the new systems – though undoubtedly "deregulated" – entail an extremely high degree of official intervention, through government agencies, the courts, the Supreme Court, even Congress. To prevent two complex multinational conglomerates which manufacture tens of thousands of items from forming an unobtrusive but illicit cartel entails an enormous machinery of constant investigation and invigilation.

The term was imported to Britain in the mid-1970s, but more by the new right than the left. Deregulation in Britain was rather different from that of the United States, although the same term was used. The UK's deregulators wanted and have very largely achieved a reform in the country's management-workforce relationships; they wanted more industry to be available for private investment; they wanted companies to serve the consumer with greater keenness, with better and more competitive products and services and at lower prices. They wanted millions of people to start accumulating shares and other property. They were trying in fact to revive the whole industrial economy by ensuring better services and supports of all kinds, especially in the newly burgeoning field of telecommunications. The term deregulation acquired wider and wider usage in their hands. It had much more to do with changing attitudes, with creating a new class of entrepreneurs, with manipulating change in society at large than had deregulation in the US.

The new Thatcher administration of the 1980s found itself dealing with an economy which was far more socialized than that of the United States and which had long lost the habits of zeal in business as these are noticeable in Japan and Germany and America. They were wanting to change in effect the prevailing belief system of British society, to make people admire entrepreneurial work and enjoy again the taking of risks through investment. Above all they wanted to rid British society of its torpor and of the influence of certain institutions, from the Coal Board and British Rail to the Post Office and the whole range of advisory quangos. For the British right in the 1980s the underlying quest was the conquest of institutions; deregulation had a very different aura from the process which had been taking place in Washington, DC.

British deregulation and the parallel policy of privatising previously publicly owned or managed enterprises were accompanied by the discovery of enterprise culture, already deeply set in the United States. In Britain it was felt that there was taking place an enthronement of self-interest with its penumbral ethics and emotions. Deregulation was an assault upon institutions, indeed, a project primarily of passionate de-institutionalization.

It seemed to the reformers that the target was the country's deep-seated practice of locking up large sectors of responsibility inside monopoly organizations which then proceeded to make up all the rules and ignore the customers. Perhaps the industry which has undergone a transformation most characteristic of the Thatcherite process is British Airways: it was sold off, slimmed down, forced to compete and go on competing, deprived of its special status, made to give up privileged access to routes and expected to smile at all its passengers; all of this it proceeded to do and few could doubt that the changes have been great and mostly beneficial.

It was the confrontation between Thatcherism and broadcasting which brought out certain contradictions lurking in the process. The Prime Minister, umbraged by what she took to be the BBC's habitual unfairness towards her government and shocked by what she took to be in ITV restrictive practices emanating from an entrenched monopoly, decided to put in hand a project of deregulatory reform. She took a step which she very rarely took during her years in office – she set up a public committee of enquiry, the seventh such enquiry in the history of British broadcasting. Unlike all its predecessors, however, the Peacock Committee was instructed to look at not the future circumstances and opportunities of radio and television but simply the fin-ances of the BBC. In other words she asked one question and one only – is there an alternative to the licence fee? The Peacock Committee's answer was "no", or rather "not yet by a long way", and in the course of giving its reasons it proceeded to examine the whole situation of broadcasting in Britain, ITV, Channel 4, cable and satellite.

The Committee was established in March 1985 and the reforms which the government finally brought about – which in the end scarcely affected the BBC – were instituted in January 1991 and only passed through Parliament just in time to meet that deadline. It was a long-fought struggle in which the supporters of high public service require-ments in commercial television gradually won back the ground inch by inch and thus left the new Independent Television Commission with a much higher level of regu-latory authority than the doctrinaire deregulators had desired or envisaged.

What has emerged is not the freewheeling public body which was originally going to impose a number of requirements upon each supplying company through contract and then ensure that it got its way, if necessary, through the courts. What has emerged is a new public institution, the ITC, watched over by the Broadcasting Standards Council with the help of the Complaints Commission; the ITC still looks to many people the spitting image of its progenitor, the IBA. There is to be an auction for the new franchises, of a kind, but only those contenders who have the right qualifications – and these are judged discretionally by the ITC – may enter the race; the highest bidder will win of course but the ITC may vary this requirement at its own discretion if one contender promises a clearly superior schedule of programmes.

What happened over the months was that a body which was to look like the American FCC, a purely regulatory, rule-applying body, turned into a broadcasting institution with powers which amount to substantial editorial discretion. The new auctions began, as the extra-Parliamentary discussions went on, to look awfully like the old ITV franchise round. There are many wholly new players, but then there always were at franchise time. It is not at all clear that the new Channel 3 will be very different from the old ITV.

Of course a number of important changes have taken place – not least the estab-lishment of a separate Radio Authority, but the Annan Committee in the 1970s had recommended that. There are some new statutory bodies set up at public expense to examine standards and complaints of unfairness but these too, are, in practice, somewhat similar to the institutions of public accountability recommended by the Annan Committee. What we saw during the post-Peacock legislative round was the slow collapse of Thatcherism as a reforming force. It was eroded not because it had run out of steam but because it simply does not fit the requirements of broadcasting – and by requirements I mean the things which society requires of broadcasting. The fact is that we all want radio and television to be regulated, including, at the end of the day, the deregulators themselves; we all want to have some kind of stake or say in this great machinery of influence over out time and our lives.

What became clear as the debate proceeded was that the more perfectly deregulation is imposed upon broadcasting, the more we lose of what viewers and legislators actually value – and that is the production of programmes which encompass a wide range of society's needs and interests. A succession of Ministers came to see that care had to be taken to keep the national programme production activity in existence, even though that meant sacrificing the nostrums of Thatcherism. Cinema in the thirties and forties had undergone an experience which had seared itself into the national psyche; American films had rapidly swept away what had been a rather healthy and diverse film-production industry in Britain. Controls and fiscal devices had been introduced to steady the situation but they all slightly misfired, unable to be of more than temporary service once the distribution industry passed into foreign control. The logic of total deregulation in British television would have been the same. And so, in the argument which went on between 1985 and 1990, more and more controls were subtly reinserted, partly in the proposed auctioning process, partly in the creation of super-visory institutions, partly in the rules governing adjacent mergers, hostile takeover, forms of compulsory programming. What was eventually, we believe, ensured is that the main businesses which distribute programmes through television channels will remain under local British indigenous control or regulation.

If you attempt to impose on broadcasting that same discipline which is very good for consumers in other industries – that is, the pressure on all prices to sink as closely as possible to costs – you get a competitive system in which the programmes are either forced to be cheap or bought in or honed down to the homogenized needs of subsidiary markets.

What Parliament and government came to understand was that it is difficult to create a transactional system in a medium which by its nature is non-transactional. It is easy to invent for viewers and listeners the label consumers, but they are not consumers of broadcasting in the normal sense of the word. Between the audience of broadcast-ing and the broadcasters there is no direct act of purchase and radio and television are social in character. They cannot ultimately be forced into being commodities.

To introduce market pressures therefore necessitated inducing the companies which supply programmes into a structure of commercial exchanges. Individual viewer choices could be made to influence them by making competition for advertising (not present previously in the UK system) take the place of normal competition between commodities. Instead of turning the programmes into the commodities which are bought and sold in a market, the would-be deregulators had to place the audience on the slab and make the suppliers bid for it, slice by slice. Of course, additional ways of supplying programmes are now possible, through cable, satellite and subscription, but these by the nature of their wares and of their technology can only be supplementary. You have to get at the bulk of the audience if you are trying to establish an open market in the medium of broadcasting, which, as the word itself suggests, is distributed by randomly scattering its wares to society as a whole.

However, competition between advertisers on simultaneous terrestrial channels (the new Channel 3 and Channel 4) would be an essential but it is not a sufficient measure of competition. That might merely have enabled the new Channel 3 companies to grow rich through holding privileged franchises, particularly since Channel 4 is limited to collecting (in competition with them) only enough advertising to survive – since it is not to have the full apparatus of shareholders and Stock Exchange quotation. So it was quite necessary to make the Channel 3 companies and all the satellite and cable companies unstable, firstly by making them guess their profits in advance through the auction, and secondly by keeping them vulnerable to takeover if they allow themselves to become cash rich. The traditional assumption in Britain that channels competing for the same audience should be prevented from competing for the same source of income cannot be maintained in a system which is seriously attempting to make commercial operations compete to live.

There was a further snag in implementing the deregulatory vision, which is that the BBC, so long as it survives, is capable of denying, as the Americans say, anything up to half of the total audience of the United Kingdom to its commercial competitors. There were well-grounded fears expressed at one point in the national post-Peacock debate that the BBC, with its ability to attract audiences with a large proportion of home-made programmes, would end up with a preponderance of viewers, while the competing commercial companies ground one another into extinction, unable to set aside sufficient revenue for programme making. The deregulatory vision is really hard to make real in a society which does not give its audiences wholeheartedly to the competitive machine. So, step by step, the vision faded and the system which has emerged can be represented as a continuation of what we have much more than it is a Thatcherite transformation.

Broadcasting's peculiar characteristics defeated the ideology. Broadcasting is social rather than transactional in character. It can be made to serve at the altar of Mr Hayek's doctrines only if it is reversed upon itself and the audiences become the goods for sales rather than the programmes. There remains, of course, the possibility of subscription becoming a good source of production finance for certain channels, but by its nature subscription entails cutting out all those members of society who are unwilling or unable to subscribe. The object of universality then has to be sacrificed and the benefits – unknown since such a system has never been tried – difficult to discern. To take the broad out of broadcasting would be like taking the yeast out of the bread. With a system based on private subscriptions for selected channels the best aspect of terrestrial television is lost; the bringing of knowledge and pleasure to everyone in any walk of station of life is sacrificed to a stifling elitism. Subscription can perhaps become a valuable specialist addition; but if it represents the heart of it, the system simply ceases to be national in scope.

One significant problem predicted by the Peacock Committee in a broadcasting system reformed along privatized and competitive lines was the need to "find means of separate and secure funding of those programmes of merit which would not survive in a market where audience rating was the sole criterion." The Committee recommended a Public Service Broadcasting Council, a governmental body to distribute money to radio and television companies in exchange for making programmes which would otherwise not be available; this was not to be an "arts and current affairs ghetto" according to the Peacock Report, which was satisfied that quite a broad range of programmes would need help of this kind. It is significant that the Committee thought that Radios 3 and 4 would also require direct funding from the PSBC. If the most eloquent and thoughtful advocates of a pure market for broadcast products believe that Radio 4 could not survive on commercial terms than how wide, I wonder, would be the range of the programmes which would be on offer in a system working entirely on subscription and competitive advertising?

In case you think that I am retreading very old territory and that the Public Service Broadcasting Council – direct government funding of individual programmes through a kind of television Arts Council – is no longer on the cards, let me refer you to a new pamphlet just published by Mr Damian Green, for the Centre of Policy Studies. While it offers firm support for a continuation of the public service principle it resurrects and enlarges Peacock's PSBC; it proposes that the PSBC be responsible for grant-aiding the production of high quality programmes all over the broadcasting system; and it wants the PSBC to be given the whole of the licence fee revenue to carry out this task. The BBC would get much of it at first but would gradually have to sit up and beg with the rest.

So if one listens very carefully one can hear today the opening chords of a new policy tune, still very much in early rehearsal. It is a new sound in deregulation policy, and it is designed to gouge out that crucial remaining element of the public broadcasting system – the financial independence conferred by the licence fee. The PSBC would be a direct quango rather than an independent broadcasting authority and according to Mr Green, for example, it would require a staff of 200 – just to carry out this task of overseeing and commissioning work from broadcasters who want to make serious and demanding programmes. Two hundred was exactly the number hired to run the whole of Channel 4 during its early years.

So the notion by which public service broadcasting is made to survive outside the framework of an independent institution still lives on but in an even more high-handed form. A source of revenue – the licence fee – which possesses among its other virtues the benefit of being non-governmental would be transmuted into government rather than viewers' money before it passed into broadcasting. Another worrying aspect of this idea is that it hands over to a non-broadcasting body decisions about what is entertainment and what is information, what can and cannot be appropriately funded by commercial means. Unfortunately it would not be unworkable. It would be rather like the Public Broadcasting System in America; I recommend anyone just to look at the kinds and quantities of paper produced to make an application for funds to one of the US endowments which support the making of documentaries and other worthy films. The process is hideously politicized and benefits only the political lobbyist for the intended product. An army of professional factors and pushers for money has inevitably been encouraged into existence – a further layer of people eating off the product. A horror. Any problem you might have experienced with Channel 4 is a picnic in comparison.

At the end of the Thatcherite era a doctrinal vacuum has developed in broadcasting, perhaps in the political agenda as a whole. It would be a tragedy if the 1990s simply continued along the same track which the previous decade had found meaningful even inspiring at times but in the end limited in its helpfulness.

Three years from now Parliament will be deciding the future – one might more accurately say the fate – of the BBC, and with it the broader issues of whether and in what form public broadcasting will survive. It is important for us all to understand that it is not the future of an industry which is at stake but the whole future of the medium. For the alterations which have been brought about during the Thatcher years in the running of commercial television are only able to exert half of their potential impact so long as the BBC, with two national channels at its disposal and a large guaranteed income, continues to attract up to half or even more of the audience.

So long as the BBC and the licence fee exist there remains a plural system in which the different elements can pursue different cultural goals, but all of them addressed to the whole audience of the United Kingdom. That, I believe, is a goal in itself, obvious though it may seem to many, and is worth fighting for. What is now at stake is the possibility of the continuation at the heart of British broadcasting of a large and effective programme producing capacity. There is a temptation built into the ITC system for franchise holders to spend less and less on programmes in order to survive in the commercial fray and in arguing for the BBC to be left fundamentally intact I am arguing for the continuation of an organization which can produce a large quantity and variety of programmes and which enjoys the tradition of political independence, strained though that has been at times over the years.

It is an odd experience to take out your battered copy of the Annan report – that neglected blueprint for broadcasting which was prepared shortly before Mrs Thatcher came into office. Much more of it has been implemented than we sometimes realize. We face the 1990s with three television institutions. Radio has its own Authority as Annan recommended. There remains a system of dual funding whereby the licence fee remains a BBC privilege and only a limited competition in advertising between Channels 3 and 4 has been permitted. The latter in its new form, as a separate institution earning its own revenue but not distributing profits to anyone is in many ways closer to the Annan plan for Channel 4 than the one Lord Whitelaw actually brought into being. Channel 5 is not yet with us but will surely acquire a unique and specialist role, based on local and regional programmes. The final outcome of the 1980s arguments, before the battle for the BBC begins, looks much like the pluralistic system of the Annan report. Even the Broadcasting Standards Council is developing along lines very reminiscent of plans put forward in the late 1970s. I am not suggesting that all we now need do is reach for those dusty, but probably well thumbed, copies of Annan. But I am suggesting that we should look again at the benefits of the plural system for at this moment we still have it and we need it more strongly than before.

One problem of the 1990s is that of getting people to believe again in the value of public institutions. These are bodies whose policies evolve with the qualities and attitudes of the nation and can be mulled over and fought over as of public right. The

BBC has long been belaboured for its haughtiness and the seemingly inexorable quality with which it carries out its self-defence. It has done much to repair this in recent years, though one cannot help feeling that if it had moved more rapidly and enthusiastically into the era of commissioning and independent programming, it would probably be in a stronger position now and have more allies within the growing industry of television.

The argument of the 1990s is necessarily an argument with the BBC as much as an argument about it. The BBC in the 1920s and 1930s was the exemplar of the public organization, the model for every quango and nationalized industry that followed. It needs today to provide the same kind of leadership in the context of our recently re-mixed economy. It has to find its own way to being prized to the point at which its political stability is reinforced. It has to offer society those qualities of responsiveness and accessibility which have become so important today, not merely in broadcasting. The BBC has, if it can find how to manage itself into the space, a very large new territory available, since the multi-channel system will not longer consist of two exclusivist camps. BBC programmes could be offered to other channels and networks. The BBC does not have to control every channel through which its programmes pass. It should see itself as the lynch-pin of a machinery of patronage. Its programmes will pass into millions of homes around the world and so back again through satellite into Britain, often in competition with BBC channels. It has the opportunity of being above channel competition; and this would also be politically helpful since the retention of the licence fee will require a demonstration that the audience spread of the BBC and of its programmes is as great in the future as in the past. The more widely the BBC is depended on the easier it will be over the decades for the licence fee to be protected and to remain a BBC dedicated form of revenue.

In the years of the 1980s we developed in this country a very narrow view of the role of democracy within the sphere of culture. We discovered the consumer. We discovered, again, the patronage of the ultra-rich. But we came to undervalue the work of all public bodies and they turned in our minds into the status of victims of a new public poverty. Whenever the Opera House, the National Theatre, the RSC, the BBC, the Arts Council made it to the front pages, it was always about the shortage of cash. These institutions, instead of being seen, by governments, sponsors and attenders, as the long-term creators of society, came to be seen merely as carping beggars, endlessly demanding for themselves a right which society no longer wanted to accord them.

I believe that it is an understanding of the role and importance of institutions themselves which may hold the key to a new stage in the broadcasting culture of this society and perhaps, of other aspects of its culture. Institutions have their own traditions and histories and imperatives; they have policies and plans which evolve over decades. They influence those who come in contact with them. Cultural institutions are the receptacles of freedom. They perform functions of influence; they can foster new tastes which then come to improve what markets have to offer.

When the shrill ideology of deregulation dies down, we are left with a television and a radio in Britain with certain specifiable needs. They need, somewhere in the landscape of the medium, some secure organizations with secure funding, not liable to be swallowed at any moment by a predatory tycoon. They need to be secured within their own professional tradition, that is, to have access to the materials of the last sixty years of broadcasting, for these are the property of the medium of broadcasting in its broadest sense. They need a large and various training ground, for experiment free of commercial pressure – not only the experiment of the young and unversed but also the experiment which only those with years of experience dare to undertake.

They need also however a new justification, not merely an argument of preservation. That new justification is not hard to find, if the BBC can begin to see itself not as an exclusive holder of channels but rather as the vast foundation of which it spoke in the 1970s. In the 1990s it should be at the centre of the system, not surviving at the periphery as the deregulators have quietly hoped. What I fear is that the government of the 1990s will try to find a place for the BBC, but a narrow and confined one. I fear that every programme maker with a vision will be made to beg like a trained animal for every scrap of funding, obliged to justify his or her thoughts to people with priorities other than programmes in their minds. I fear that the BBC will be made to survive but under occupation by accountants and if not accountants then civil servants. Those are the fears.

There are also hopes. One is that a new kind of debate over broadcasting will characterize the 1990s in which we concentrate on looking for organizational techniques which will enable programme making to proceed in conditions which support intellectual independence. I hope also that the BBC will now lead the debate and not duck it as it has done throughout the 1980s. It has much to offer, not only behind locked doors, and that is principally its own history and heritage. I hope also that the programme makers will not all be transformed into a class of small businesses but will see their task as that of developing their skills to provide to provide knowledge and delight, some of it for profit and some of it with no motive other than the pleasure of communication.

·   ·   ·

A short discussion followed the speech. Questions were raised about: the world role of the BBC; the enhancement of democracy within the BBC and ways in which it might be made more publicly accountable; the impact of new technology, and the role of the BBC in serving local communities. Among those who contributed to the discussion were:

Jim Brown, consultant
John Forrest, National Transcommunications
Gillian Reynolds, *Daily Telegraph*
David Rushton, Institute of Local Television
Michael Starks, BBC
Bryan Waddington, Communications Commission
Mark Wheeler, University of London

2 Programmes: Implications of change

Andrea Wonfor
Controller, Arts & Entertainment, Channel 4 Television Company

Michael Braham
Chief Executive, Broadcast Communications

Roger Bolton
Head of Network Features, Thames Television

Chair: Mary McAnally
Head of Features, Thames Television

Mary McAnally: We are going to run this session as a debate. The future of the BBC is, of course, an enormous, thought-provoking and important subject and it may seem strange to any BBC staff members at the Symposium that this session has as its guests three well-known figures in broadcasting, none of whom is currently working at the BBC. This is intentional, as we are going to try and stand back and take an outsider's look at the BBC. We shall also try to talk about how any changes to the BBC may affect the rest of us working either in ITV companies or at Channel 4 or the independent sector or, indeed, in satellite channels.

Now, can I just describe the structure of the session? We are going to use subject headings and I shall go to the panel each time and then come to the audience. First we shall talk about the importance of the BBC, how the panel see the BBC; the importance of the BBC as a corner-stone of our culture. Next, I shall ask each of our broadcasting experts for their views on the implications of change to the BBC. We shall look at what happens if the Government keeps the licence fee the same, what happens if it reduces the licence fee, the impact of possible advertising, the impact of sponsorship and pay per view and then the possibility of splitting the BBC up into various parts.

Andrea Wonfor: I've never had the privilege of working for the BBC and because this is a warm-up session for much weightier debates to come, I hope that everybody at this session will go along with how I read it, which is at least to kick some ideas around and perhaps say some fairly extreme things and perhaps some prejudiced things.

I was on a judging panel recently for the Royal Television Society in arts programmes

15

and watching a very clever reconstruction of Virginia Woolf's lecture at Girton on *A Room of One's Own*, in which she was arguing, among other things, that in order to be creative one needed a fixed income of a certain amount and a room of one's own. It only occurred to me, thinking about this session, that that is behind my idea of the BBC. I feel that, over the years, there has evolved a kind of core complacency in the BBC because they have had, since 1927 I think, the privilege of a licence fee, a fixed income, a reliable income, and, if not a room of their own, a place in the sun, a place in British culture. And, as a result of that privilege, they went on, as Virginia Woolf went on, to do some rather wonderful creative things and became, certainly until the creation of ITV, a template, a corner-stone for what broadcasting could achieve in terms of educating and entertaining and informing.

But that's where I have a certain outsider's resentment of this fact because I think it has been ably demonstrated since ITV got under way that the BBC does not have a monopoly on talent, ideas and innovation. Since the creation of Channel 4 and the growth of the independent sector, it has been amply demonstrated that all those elements which we value in the BBC's output are achievable by other means, by other sources of funding, by other ways of talent coming together, by other dynamics.

That said, I feel that the BBC will have an increasingly important part to play as the nineties progress. Let me explain that. Since ITV and Channel 4 are about to enter somewhat uncharted waters as market forces come into play over the next two or three or four years, it is important for British broadcasters and the British public to decide what they want of an institution which represents public service broadcasting and all that it stands for. It is extremely important to make a commitment that will relate to the three years between 1993 and 1996, when the licence fee will be reviewed. We should make a commitment to sustaining what I don't like to think of as a corner-stone exactly, but at least an area of National Trust property.

I agree with some of the things that Michael Checkland said recently. I do think that British broadcasting needs a public service core which provides a critical mass for innovation, risk-taking, for training, and I think that core has to extend beyond factual programmes. My definition for public service broadcasting is not narrow at all. I'm always reminding people that Channel 4's entertainment and comedy programming and so on are part of Channel 4's remit too, but you do need constant innovation. *Network Seven*, for instance, set a very good example because it provided such interesting ways of putting factual programmes across that it has had an effect on the way that mainstream current affairs programmes are handled. The BBC should be seen in that way across the board in all areas of programming, the lighter weight entertainment areas of broadcasting should be seen as very much part of public service broadcasting.

In the longer term, beyond 1996, the BBC will have a very important role if one looks twenty or thirty or forty years ahead, as the regional broadcaster for Britain

If one looks in the context of the EEC and the global television environment, I think it is going to be extremely important in the way that for me, regional broadcasting in the North-East of England at its best was able to reflect that area's culture back to itself, and create forums for particular debates and particular interests which only existed between the Tyne and the Tees. The BBC, or whatever it is going to be called in in thirty or forty years' time, should be safeguarded as a forum for regional, English, British – whatever one calls it – television in the future. That, for me, is the long-term important function of public service broadcasting in this country.

One could go on and talk about the limitations that one would think one should impose on the BBC as it starts examining itself. It has to focus more clearly on what its role should be but other sessions will deal with that. The short-term importance of the BBC is to safeguard certain commitments which I'm sure most of the British public would back, and I think all broadcasters would back, and the Government, if it had got any sense, would back in terms of the role of having a critical mass broadcaster, particularly when there are great changes going on in other areas of broadcasting, whereas in the long-term it must represent, very forcibly, a voice for British culture in thirty or forty year's time.

Michael Braham: I agree with all that and I hope we are not going to agree about everything. Andrea constantly talks about the long-term but my perspective is that of the independent producer trying to make a living. We have no certainty of revenue, we have no licence fee, we have no monopoly of advertising, we have no sort of levy and, I'm afraid, for us the long-term means "not in this financial year."

I was brought into television by somebody called John Birt who was then at London Weekend Television and who is now quite important in the BBC, but my own direct personal experience of the BBC is quite limited. When I first left Thames and set up as an independent I did some work on a series called *All Our Working Lives*, a BBC documentary series, which was quite an interesting education. It was the sort of series that may never get made again because it was about a domestic subject, it was an expensive, ambitious series, and the sort of programme that is going to be very, very hard to fund in any way in the future. One of the insights I gained into the BBC at that time was its extraordinary way of looking at its own finances which I think has changed to an extent since then, in that resources – facilities, people and so on – of which the BBC had a lot, were thought of as being there anyway and, in a sense, free, whereas money where you have to write a cheque and send it to somebody was thought of in a completely different way. For example, if you wanted to keep the cutting room going as Peter Pagnamenta normally did for three months more, or have a researcher for a year, that was not important but if you wanted fifty pounds in cash, that was impossible. I think the BBC has come quite a long way to seeing the world in more realistic terms but there is perhaps still some way to go.

As I said, my perspective is that of an independent producer and perhaps I should just briefly say what the BBC means to us as suppliers at the moment. We are, according to the famous Television Week survey, the second biggest independent producer. We, in turn, have relatively recently become part of a bigger group which I ought to mention since we are here in Manchester, which is The Guardian and Manchester Evening News plc. This, of course, includes the Manchester Evening News and various other media interests in this region. Last year we supplied a total of twenty hours of programming to the BBC which included, for example, *Food and Drink* from Basil Productions, one of our companies, which is a high-rating programme on BBC 2, and another of our companies, Hawkshead, had a repeat of the Roux brothers' cookery series and also provided programmes for *Job Bank* which is careers advice for young people. Now twenty hours is quite a lot of programming and it's a lot more than we provided to ITV at that time but it was, in our case, out of a total of 283 hours during the year so though the BBC is an important customer we feel there's a long way to go there still. In addition to those twenty hours we are responsible for the televising of the House of Commons and, of course, the BBC is one of the many customers for that.

So we see the BBC as a very important customer and we would like to see it becoming a more important customer. From the independent perspective I think this is going to be one of the main themes of the next few years. The BBC has still a long way to go to meet its twenty-five per cent quota, and, as you will have seen, the pace is beginning to speed up a little bit with, for example, the idea of putting *Question Time* out to independents. This is something we want to encourage and see develop, more particularly at a time when Channel 4 is probably going to have a standstill in terms of revenue and when television in general, where it is advertising-related, is having to cut back.

The other importance of the BBC – and the reason I do think that it is something to be nurtured – is to do with risk-taking, to do with being able to persist when things are not an immediate success and there have been lots of examples of that. *Blackadder* was one example where the first series was not terribly successful but there was the ability, because of the secure funding, and, perhaps, because of the two channels, to stay with it and to develop what became an extremely successful series. I would be extremely sorry to see that going. So in the future the public service element is going to be more and more important, particularly because with the forthcoming auction of ITV Channel 3 licences, there is no question that Channel 3 companies, having paid away a very high proportion of their future revenue for the licences, are going to have to be more popular in their approach, are going to have less scope for the kind of factual programming, the documentaries, the news that we all think is very important. The role of the BBC, as the beacon in this area, is going to be increasingly important.

Roger Bolton: It is very difficult for me to be objective. It is rather like someone looking back to a failed marriage and trying to tell you what actually happened. So, I can't be objective.

It took a disgracefully long time to realize that the BBC is not important in itself but as a means to an end. One of the things that got lost in the mid-eighties was a clear view within the corporation of what the BBC is for. Now, I notice that a large number of study groups are being set up to find the holy grail of what is the BBC for. It does bear a rather curious comparison with John Major's attempt to discover an alternative to the poll tax. Again, I'm not entirely objective about this; there's a sense of let-down from the BBC in the last three or four years. I thought, twenty years ago anyway, that one of the justifications for the BBC being funded by the public was that it would represent, to some extent, the public's interests as against the Government. This may, indeed, have been a naive thought, given the nature of the funding, but it seems to me one of the sadnesses of the last three years, for which the Government bears at least as much responsibility as the BBC, is that the BBC has become, in some ways, simply the biggest company in broadcasting.

Is it the leader of public service broadcasting? It is not the moral leader, it is not the leading voice in terms of independence. That may be a role which has been taken over by Channel 4. Certainly those of us in ITV who were trying to argue in the last three years against simply the highest bid taking over would have greatly appreciated not the interference of the BBC but a very clear statement that British broadcasting has a delicate balance and that if you change one element in it you affect the others. That didn't happen and therefore, if one does not detect a great deal of warmth from me for the BBC as an institution, I think it is not surprising.

Nonetheless, it remains absolutely central to the future of programming in this country and, therefore, however reluctantly, one wishes to see it survive until the moment arrives when a different or better way can be found of achieving the ends that it is supposed to bring about.

There are a number of reasons why I think it should be important. At the very simplest level I, for one, would simply like to watch programmes with no ads in. I'd like to watch complete programmes. I'd like to be able to make a programme on anti-semitism which does not have to break for ads for *TV Quick*. I would also like it to survive because, with the secure funding which it has as opposed to anyone else in broadcasting, it is able to make long term commitments to programmes, the sort of commitments that are becoming almost impossible in ITV.

For example, two years ago, we made a programme on Stalin – three programmes, three one-hours, two years' work. I can't tell you how much it cost. I can tell you how much money went out in cash terms but in terms of the internal resources, I couldn't tell you. But now I can tell you what everything will cost in Thames. And I can now tell you that we'll never make a series like that again. We may make a series about Stalin; it will certainly be co-produced with America as this one was but it will have to be very, very substantially reduced in terms of resources.

If you want an example of the way ITV is going, you want to pop down to the reception area of Manchester's Granada Television and pick up a copy of its magazine, which is called *The Leader* (I am sure that's a public relations mistake). But, anyway, on the front page you read what the Leader is telling the whole of the team in Granada. "A competitive schedule," says Andrew Quinn, the Managing Director, "makes the best use of the best material, plays to those shows which are already established successes. We quite happily throw away slots at the moment. For example we schedule known low-audience current affairs shows in prime slots thereby creating some slots for the opposition to schedule against. We commission high-price drama and play it against established successes on the BBC." Later on he says, "If current producers aspire to high audiences, as all producers do, they will have to look to the nature of the shows that they make. In future they could themselves on the periphery of the schedule. But I believe they will understand that current affairs produced in a particular way and scheduled at the right availability to view period, become marketable programming." And at the end of it the Director of Programmes, Steve Morrison, says that he wants to get 50 per cent of the audience, not 43 per cent, and, secondly that "peak time should no longer be regarded as that which lies between 6 o'clock and 10.30pm."

The writing is on the wall for what is going to happen to ITV once the new franchises are out. It has been a tough enough battle up to now to preserve a mixed sort of programming in peak. It may well be that this proves impossible in ITV and it will only, therefore, be in television terms the BBC, and BBC 1, that will have it.

In any case, one of the crucial arguments for the BBC has been this relationship between the two main channels. ITV factual programmes of a certain age have only been in peak because the BBC, with *Panorama* at 9.30, takes its punishment, if you like, in audiences in its turn. Not a great punishment: *World in Action* and *This Week* average something between five and seven million depending on the time of year, whether we are in a war or not. In the past this balance has been maintained by the two channels. And, to some extent, a balance is maintained by Channel 4 and BBC 2.

I think there are threats also in terms of Channel 4. I don't expect Andrea to accept it is as large a risk as I think it is. But, undoubtedly, with the changes in the Broadcasting Act which mean that Channel 4 has to raise it own revenue, it is probably going to go for higher audiences, and needs to do so. If, at the same time, ITV is scheduling against it, if, indeed, ITV intends to get 50%, you can see the sort of situation that will develop. This will present the BBC with a very difficult problem. At its best, the BBC's role will become more important because it may be the only channel in BBC 1 which presents a mixed schedule. It may also be, of course, the BBC loses its nerve as its audiences drops and, under great pressure, finds itself in some trouble. So the BBC has always been terribly important in maintaining that balance in broadcasting. There's a good chance that it may be even more important in the future as the rest of us pursue audiences.

There's another way in which, for me as a journalist working in television, it's been terribly important to have the BBC there. We legitimize each other. If only one channel does a certain type of programming, raises a certain type of question, it can be said that the editor of those programmes, or the reporters, are merely obsessed, particularly if the Government of the day, or even the Front Benches together, are saying that certain issues are not important. If at least two programmes, or three programmes, are covering broadly the same area, or asking some of the same questions, it legitimizes the activity. That is something that may come under threat, and it is another reason why it's extremely important to maintain competition. I've always thought it rather curious that this Government believes in competition, except as far as public service broadcasting is concerned. It seems to me if you believe in competition, you should believe in competition in that as much as in anything else.

The BBC clearly lays central. There's one other thought I have. Please, BBC, don't become even more metropolitan than you are. The revenue is raised throughout the country. You speak to the whole country, or you ought to. The regional and local broadcasting of the BBC, to my mind, is as important as the network programming itself. This may not be a popular view, certainly for those who wish to lop off local radio. But what we see in television at the moment is the increasing difficulty of making programmes solely for our own audience. You ask ITV, or BBC, or Channel 4 at the moment, how many expensive, domestic series, serious factual series dealing with this country they can fully fund, and the answer is one per year – virtually nil. You'll find the funding is increasingly 40 or 60 or 80% and, therefore, if there is no significant sales potential or network production potential, that series will, odds on, not get made. There are benefits; there are a lot of good international series, but we are already in a position where we have lost our independence as British programme makers when it comes to making expensive series about Britain. The BBC ought to admit that in order to look at its priorities and wonder whether it should not move back to fully funding such series rather than some of the other things that it's involved in. But that's what at stake.

The BBC is extraordinarily important and will remain so for the next four or five years. But it has to prove that it is the best means to achieve the end we want which should be a service which does occasionally surprise, which is available to all, which does cater for minorities, which introduces people to subjects and areas they might not have thought of while giving them good, interesting and entertaining programming that the majority want to watch. It should be a service which is independent of Government and leads the argument for the freedoms which all broadcasters would want to cherish. There's a question mark in my mind about whether it can continue to do that so I hope that the BBC's study groups are more successful than John Major's looks as though they are going to be.

Mary McAnally: Can we now go on and talk about 1996 – the possible changes that might happen to the BBC, what the panel thinks about how this will affect the BBC and how will that, in turn, affect the rest of us; what will the knock-on be? Can we talk about the licence fee and either that the licence fee could remain the same, bearing in mind that it is this year three points under the retail price index, or that the Government could decide to keep it the same as the retail price index in 1996 – or it could reduce it? What effect does the panel think that this will have on the BBC and, in turn, on the rest of broadcasting?

Michael Braham: Licence fees are wonderful things, aren't they? My daughter, who is a student, is moving out of college into a house and she has to get a television licence for the first time: £77, you know, is quite a chunk of money. The current situation, as I understand it, is that although the last rise was below inflation, rises from now until 1996 will be at the rate of inflation.

This is a dream, isn't it? Can you imagine? You are asked to run a business with revenues of about £1200 million and inflation-proofed for the next five years. It should be so easy and I can't see how anybody would want to complain about that. However, there are a few problems within that: one is that there is inflation and inflation. There is the rise in prices that everybody else pays and then there are the rise in prices that we have to pay in broadcasting which, of course, are much higher for some reason. It has been used for years, that, and you could argue that it is pretty outrageous to hide behind that.

However, there is some reality there and it probably will get worse in that the price of talent, of people who are actually going to appear on screen, is going to go up because we are going to have more channels and we are going to have more competition between the channels. If you are ambitious this is the way to go: get on screen, because you are going to earn an awful lot of money. So to some extent it's true that the rate of inflation of broadcasting costs will be higher than the general rate of inflation. The BBC will have to cope with that. Of course if the licence fee is reduced, which I think is pretty unlikely, that will exaggerate the effect.

21

There is going to be pressure on costs and the question of whether it operates as efficiently as it might will continue to be raised. Clearly this is something that concerns the BBC, and they have all kinds of working parties looking at these things rather slowly and perhaps not as radically as they might. I don't know if one is allowed to mention John Harvey Jones but he had certain criticisms of the BBC which you will recall – for example, that it had far too many bureaucrats and twice as many top managers as it needed. Clearly these are the things which ought to be addressed and I am sure, if the licence fee stays the same, they will be addressed; if it is reduced there is no question about it.

Picking up something Roger said, it may be desirable that the BBC doesn't become more metropolitan but I think it is inevitable. I am sure a lot of the cuts will come out of the regions and not just out of radio. I am sure we will see the BBC become a more metropolitan service in the future as part of this squeeze that I am describing.

In case I forget to mention it later there is one thing that ought to be said about the BBC. We worry about it and grumble about it and fret about how much it costs but a delegation was over here recently from South Korea which, now it's got rich, has decided to create its own BBC because they think it's such a wonderful institution that they would like to have one too. It's an interesting perspective, isn't it, that this is seen as being something extremely desirable and something that they would like to emulate?

Roger Bolton: The crazy licence fee is the most wonderfully efficient system of getting the best programmes on the air and getting most programmes on to the screen. The problem is how you stop the BBC becoming complacent about it. I think the licence fee deal is an exceptionally good one. But you have got to judge that deal in relationship with what is happening in the rest of the market. And, of course, the rest of the market is disastrous; it is having the worst time for at least ten years. Programme cuts would have been far more extensive in ITV if it hadn't been the franchise application year at the time because the consequences of the recession in terms of revenue have been disastrous. There is not exactly going to be a haemorrhaging of talent from the BBC, although one hears there is a rather large number of BBC names on the franchise applications; but only a certain number of people can win the franchises. So the BBC is going to be in a better financial position than either ITV or Channel 4 in the next two or three years.

After that it is difficult to say what will happen to the recession. When will the election be, what will be the attitude? I think it's got a very good deal. I hope that it doesn't sit back and wait and think "we're all right for the moment." It must continue its defining process of what it's about. All the economic logic, however, is to cut back to the centre. But then, if you do that, one of the reasons for a poll tax, which in a way is what the BBC licence fee is, is taken away. Why should you pay in Newcastle or elsewhere? What does it give you back? Does it give you a job? The BBC at its peril cuts back on its local and regional programming. Besides which, why can't they simply ship out of London a whole department? I mean this idea of the guy who used to edit quite a lot of current affairs from Manchester when Monica Sims was Controller of Radio 4. I'm being unfair to a very intelligent lady but she did say that it was axiomatic that all network national current affairs programmes had to be produced from London and she said "Michael, if you go abroad, you have to come through London Airport." Michael did explain that there was rather a large airport down the road here.

In the age of fax, why does everything have to be based upon London? There are significant cost savings to be made elsewhere and if you have a significant investment in network talent out of London, that feeds two ways: one, it feeds out towards the people doing the regional and local programming and two, the ideas of those doing local and regional programming feed back in to the mainstream and enrich it.

Mary McAnally: So you think that if the licence fee remains the same the BBC won't have to cut anything or trim anything?

Roger Bolton: It's having to make some cuts but they are not significant compared to what's going on elsewhere and the crucial thing will be the Election.

Mary McAnally: Right. And you are for shipping regional stuff out?

Roger Bolton: If the Revenue can do it I can't see why the BBC can't.

Michael Braham: The idea of moving out of London is laudable but, given that the top staff at the BBC won't move from Broadcasting House to Shepherds Bush, I think you've got a lost cause there.

Andrea Wonfor: I was saddened that the BBC had to be chased by Mrs Thatcher and her cohorts into the position it is now in of reviewing itself. Given the assembled brain power in the BBC, it is extraordinary that in the early eighties they had not some way moved themselves to contemplate the more competitive future without the Tories having to tell them.

I remember talking to Janet Street Porter when she first joined the BBC and I asked her "How's it going, Janet?". She said "There's so many men in grey suits". She quoted this recently at a Spot the Difference Conference on women in television as did John Birt in his opening address to the same meeting when he said that he had to confess to the assembled room that every time that he saw a room full of men in grey suits at the BBC he kept thinking that half of them should be replaced by equally able women. John Birt's problem, of course, is that he has got to get rid of 50% of them first before he replaces 25% of that number with able women.

Roger Bolton: Of course, really, he could get rid of himself and put a woman in his place.

Andrea Wonfor: It would not be a bad thing if one looked hard at the licence fee being certainly the same, possibly reduced because one has got to keep the pressure up on the BBC, as there is a danger of complacency. Although I'm in favour of regional broadcasting, if there is great emphasis upon ITV companies providing regional broadcasting, and if Channel 5 is seriously going to look at regional broadcasting to some areas of the country, it takes some of the weight off the BBC and I don't think the BBC can do everything all the time. I do agree, though, that moving centres of production out is an extremely good thing.

I'm all for lopping off bits of the BBC. I think it should look at new ideas. It should look at Radios 1 and 2. It should look at the bulk of its regional programming and what it does. Some of it isn't that good, some of it is very good, some of it finds its way on to the national screens and helps create texture and lets different voices be heard nationally. I think there is a job for the BBC to help the nation talk to itself more.

Roger Bolton: It has made changes already. It has struck down its regional features programmes, arguably the wrong decision, in order to invest as much as it can in news of which I think they'll need to cut back in the future or create a further problem. But the problem about Radio 1 and 2 is, as you know, is that the amount that of money that you save by doing that is very small.

Andrea Wonfor: One starts looking at the different ways of doing things, the numbers of people you need to administrate and sort out contracts and so on, and my impression is that there are layers and layers and layers of that going on in the BBC. Cutting it is not easy and it has to be done in a humanitarian way; it can't happen overnight. But I do think that the BBC needs to examine itself, to ask itself what it should be doing, and that is why I raised questions about radio and regional programming and so on; everything should be debated.

I think the core activity of the BBC is texture, a mixed schedule, quality, excellence, innovation, all those things. You have to work out what you need to achieve that and everything else should be under question.

Michael Braham: We keep talking about the regions. The BBC spends something like £280 million in the regions, including radio, which is about 50% more than the entire cost of Channel 4 programmes. This is an enormous sum, and hardly justifiable.

Mary McAnally: Can I move on now to the next point? In 1996 it could be, as everyone knows, that the government may decide that the licence fee isn't the sole provider for the BBC and allow advertising, subscription or pay per view, and I'll put all three together, because time is against us. Roger Bolton, from an ITV viewpoint, what do you make of that?

Roger Bolton: Disaster. It is clearly the view of the advertisers at the moment that a majority would go straight to the BBC to advertise. It depends how much advertising they were allowed to put on the BBC, but they would assess that on the whole BBC 1, because it has an ideal audience, younger and with more ABC1s etc. than ITV, although that's changing a bit, is very attractive, and therefore they will be very keen to maximize the amount of opportunities they have on BBC 1. You're then left with the question of what would be left of ITV.

Of course in the end if it's an absolute choice between survival or death, the BBC will take advertising. It would be extremely bad for everyone else, but I think the government would understand that and that's why I think they would crawl back in the end. I think it would be a disaster if it did happen, and above all I think a disaster for the viewer; if we had to have pay per view to be able to watch programmes without interruption, what a reduction in the quality broadcasting that would be. I believe the licence fee will remain the central funding for the BBC, as long as the BBC is thought to be central to the broadcasting in this country.

Michael Braham: This is the problem with the licence fee. It is very easy to see why it is a bad idea as a poll tax and so on, but when you talk about what it could be replaced with, you're on very shaky ground. After the experience of the abolition of the rates, and coming in with a different kind of system, I would have thought any government would be rather cautious in this area. The one real argument in favour of moving the BBC to advertising or subscription is that potentially it might free it from the direct political pressure of having the licence fee under government control and the government being able to turn the screw all the time. But a mixture of advertising and licence fee would be very hard to sustain and it would have to be one or the other.

In other countries the idea that there is a sort of equilibrium that can be reached between being part commercial and part funded by a poll tax is an uneasy one.

The immediate effect of bringing advertising into the BBC would be that all the people who are currently applying for Channel 3 licences would take the government to court on the grounds that they have been sold a complete crock. They would say that they had bought their new licences – 10 year licences – in a situation where the BBC doesn't take advertising, and then if the government introduces advertising that would be rather difficult for them.

There is a public demand for watching programmes uninterrupted; this has been demonstrated to an extent in the United States not only by public television, but also by the big cable companies where people will pay to watch movies uninterrupted rather than have them broken up every few minutes by advertising.

Subscription is a completely different thing. If you take advertising you're not restricting the availability of the programme, but as soon as you talk about a subscription system, you are cutting off a lot of people – on the first day, almost everybody, because it would take some time for people to acquire the equipment. Some people would never be able to acquire the equipment or pay the fees and the nature of the service is that it could no longer be a public service station because many people wouldn't be able to receive it. Pay per view is a refinement of that, but the same arguments apply. You simply knock a hole in the whole structure of public service broadcasting if you go down the subscription route. Subscription for a new service, as has been talked about overnight on the BBC, is a different thing, but actually to turn over the existing channels to subscription won't win any votes.

Andrea Wonfor: Roger is worried about the future of Channel 4 selling its own air time. We are feeling very bullish about it; we think we target audiences rather well and our share is going up. My heart goes out to franchise applicants who are trying to work out what money they are going to make over the next 10 years and so on, but the projections I've seen for Channel 4 provided we keep our share healthy make it look like we will be very viable by the end of the century. But nobody really knows, so the thought of saying now, yes to advertising on some or part or all of the BBC seems crazy; the only winners will be the advertisers. On the other hand, who knows? Between now and 1995, if things go much better than everyone has projected, and we come out of the recession and into boom time, there may well be a swell of opinion in favour of advertising on the BBC that appears as a renewed force.

As far as pay per view is concerned, it immediately starts excluding people or they give you second hand goods, even if you do give a recorded highlight, and as far as subscription goes I'm sure there is a drop-out factor – people, including myself, forget to renew their Sky movie card or perhaps they find they start and then can't afford it.

So I would hope that none of those routes have to be gone down in terms of finding survival money for the BBC; I think we should slowly look at some of those things, see what technology makes possible and so on, and that's another territory that we can probably look at towards the end of the nineties but don't rush.

Mary McAnally: What if sponsorship were allowed only on BBC 2?

Andrea Wonfor: I could argue in some ways that one of the things we ought to knock off the BBC is BBC 2, and ensure the healthy survival of Channel 4, but of course we need the competition. You need it to have an energy that comes from two or three channels doing the same thing.

Mary McAnally: In 1996 if the government is going to split bits of the BBC away and privatize them, which bits do you think they should hive off?

Michael Braham: The BBC has tended to have the feeling that it has to be all things to all men, and cover everything. We have the famous example of coming in at breakfast time ahead of TV-am which some would argue wasn't really necessary, then the local radio, on which I know there are different views, and – a great example – the DBS, direct broadcasting by satellite, project where the BBC blew away £10 million before it realized that it wasn't viable. This attitude has got to change, and the BBC should concentrate more on the things that it used to concentrate on. Whether having five channels of radio is really necessary as part of the BBC is open to question, and I think those are the areas most suitable perhaps to be sold off or voted off. I would personally be very sorry to see one of the TV channels go, for reasons we talked about at the beginning to do with the flexibility and risk taking that the BBC can do with two channels which it would no longer be able to do with one. That one channel would have to be a more popular channel to compete and a lot of the public service elements would necessarily be squeezed out.

Andrea Wonfor: I have to agree on radio. But that doesn't mean to say I don't think radio is excellent, but I think there is a logic to looking at why the BBC should do radio as well. I can't see why the BBC has to be in local programming unless very radically, such as by fostering independent production all over the British Isles, but I don't think it necessarily has to be the BBC that is providing local programming all that way So I would go for radio, local programming, service sectors and on reflection maybe BBC 2.

Mary McAnally: You don't mean that, do you?

Andrea Wonfor: No. We need something to keep us on our toes.

Roger Bolton: Does the BBC have to be in there? It has to be in there as long as we are not persuaded that a function that we think is worthwhile cannot be provided by any other means. It doesn't mean that BBC necessarily does well in every area. One has to recognize that the only reason the BBC has moved in a number of areas is because of very tough external pressure, so even if you decide as I hope that a lot of the functions would be retained we do have to look at the way the BBC itself provides or fulfils them. If you look at the Radio 4 example, I would like to see to what extent it was possible for commercial radio in some form to provide competition there. I don't think it can. Until it is demonstrated that that is going to happen, we wouldn't move on Radio 4.

Nonetheless if you look at Radio 4, it has the feeling of a stodgy channel. There are a vast number of unproductive producers involved and a lot of the areas could do desperately with a breath of fresh air. The problem is that they are not going to get it at the moment, or we're not going to get as good a service which is really a problem elsewhere.

The question is how do you change the culture within the BBC, and in order to fulfil its remit, what does the BBC need to have in terms of bureaucracy, what does it need to have in terms of facilities, how many programmes must be produced in house? You could come up with a lot of radical answers there. If you take out some of the function you save virtually nothing in terms of money but you lose something perceived as being valuable without proof that what is provided can be provided by somebody else.

Mary McAnally: My last point, to spring it on the panel, is on the actual programmes the BBC is putting out at the moment. Over the nineties do you want any changes?

Andrea Wonfor: I'll speak as a viewer; I'll try and be objective about it. I think I would like to see some slightly more experimental work going on in comedy and so on on the BBC. Although they are doing some rather good material at the moment they never quite go that little bit further, in the sense that we tend to trawl around, we feel that Channel 4 take risks with unknown people who then do a couple of good series and disappear off to BBC 2 and do very good work for them. I would like to see them feeding us with some new faces now and again. I would like some fresher entertainment formats to come through and for another *Mastermind* format to be discovered, but generally I wouldn't put my finger on anything major. I am happy with the competition the way it is, thank you.

Michael Braham: In the area of factual programming they've gone through a big change, with John Birt's reorganizations. They've tightened things up and in many ways do a more thorough job now, but I think I would like to see some more risk-taking coming back, with more controversial programmes and perhaps more investigative programmes because there are going to be fewer and fewer of them on Channel 3 is going to find ... these things are going to be less and less on Channel 3, pushed more and more to the fringes of the schedule, and this is where the public service broadcaster comes into its own.

Roger Bolton: I wish somebody anywhere would find good new sitcom. In the factual area, I think two things. First of all, the BBC should become less cautious. There used to be a philosophy in the BBC twenty or thirty years ago which went roughly like this: it is not for the BBC to establish the borders of debate; that is for parliament and for others; it is for the BBC once those borders have been established to investigate most thoroughly. That is an entirely limiting role. That effectively is what the BBC has been about in the last three years. In the current affairs areas, there is a narrowing of the range of views. Although there is difficulty with the impartiality, the great danger if you don't have plenty of room for opinion, on the right as well as the left, is that you narrow the agenda, and we also do the same agenda and anybody who is trying to get in new thoughts into the political process or the political debate is denied access. So I would like to see more *One Pairs Of Eyes*, more vigorous expression of opinion, a widening of the area of debate, and less clustering at the centre of the agenda, a strengthening of the investigation and that's all.

. . .

Points were made from the floor at various stages in the panel discussion.

One speaker suggested that Michael Checkland (director-general of the BBC) would have been very happy to hear the panellists speak, since they were all defending the existence of the licence fee rather than exploring alternatives.

There was opposition from the floor to the idea of privatizing BBC radio, on the grounds that these services were also complementary to those of commercial radio, and that they provided advertising-free listening.

It was pointed out that the audience for BBC TV current affairs was the same size as that for Radio 4, and Radio 4 was not a service that would be provided by commercial radio. It was repeated that no-one had yet come up with a viable alternative to the licence fee. If put against the costs of a single subscription to Sky Movies the licence fee was a bargain.

Another speaker pointed out that the BBC receives less revenue than ITV and Channel 4 combined, and yet with that revenue it produces two television channels, five national radio channels and local radio. It would be naive to suggest that the BBC could get rid of a few people in grey suits and save significant money.

It was pointed out that whatever changes were made there would still be a licence fee. Few people really complained about paying their gas, electricity or telephone bills; only politicians and broadcasters were worried about the licence fee.

It had been suggested in research that 80% of the population would be willing to pay a subscription to the BBC; but if this were so it would have to be instituted at once rather than at a time when the BBC had become debilitated by a lack of money, because there would be much less willingness to subscribe to a weak BBC. In any case, said another speaker, if most of the population were willing to pay for the BBC, what would be the point of changing the system?

A representative of the BBC declared himself encouraged by what had been said. He said that if the BBC expressed the amount of the licence fee in monthly terms and collected it itself then it would be seen that there was a lot of life in it yet. The BBC should not only be efficient but should demonstrate its efficiency. There should be a shared understanding between the BBC and the public as to what it is for.

On the other hand, another speaker expressed his amazement that the world was so full of people who thought that money dropped from the sky. The evidence showed that when the licence fee went up it was unpopular, and that the larger it got the more unpopular it was. A voluntary tax might be more popular, but it was unlikely to work.

Participants in the discussion included:

Steven Barnett, Henley Centre
John Gray, consultant
Jocelyn Hay, Voice of the Listener
Chris Horsley, Yorkshire Television

Barbara Hosking, Yorkshire Television
Harold Lind, consultant
Pam Mills, consultant
David Rumble, PA Consulting Group
David Rushton, Institute of Local Television
Michael Starks, BBC
Carole Stone, freelance broadcaster

3 Advertising on the BBC

Libby Child
Director, Young & Rubicam Advertising

Gillian Laidlaw
Kinsley Lord Management Consultants

Harold Lind
Consultant

Richard Wade
Director-General, Advertising Association

Chair: Cresta Norris
TV-am

Cresta Norris: This is just a brief introduction to give you some sense of the question of the BBC taking advertising. I don't need to tell you that the nineties are going to see some dramatic changes in British broadcasting. The Broadcasting Act of 1990 has meant the relicensing of ITV and Channel 4 becoming an independent corporation. There are possibilities in Channel 5 and issues of cable, satellite and video sell-through.

The BBC hasn't up till now had to worry very much about these changes because it has been protected by a Royal Charter. In fact it has had six Royal Charters over the past 60 years and the current one is up for review in 1996. The BBC's purpose is defined by a licence and agreement from the Home Secretary which requires impartiality. But there have been seven enquiries into British broadcasting since 1923. The most recent was the Peacock enquiry reported in 1986 on options for financing the BBC. His main recommendation was that the BBC should move towards a subscription service, and he put the case against advertising on the BBC.

Now this year the Home Office commissioned a report from Price Waterhouse, a firm of consultants, and it was used by the Home Secretary as one reason why the licence fee increase from 1991 should be set at less than the rate of inflation. The licence fee is presently fixed at 3% below the rate of inflation and this means that the BBC is probably going to have to cut its costs by about 10% over the next five years. So the question in front of us is: is there going to be enough money to fund BBC 1 and BBC 2, specific programmes for local audiences produced in Northern Ireland, Scotland, Wales, the five English regions, five national radio stations, and 37 local radio stations? And if there isn't enough money to fund them, will there be job cuts within the BBC? Or is there some merit in supplementing the licence fee with advertising? It is worth pointing out that the people who pay less for their licence fees in Germany, Switzerland, Ireland, France, Italy and the Netherlands are all supplemented by advertising. So those are the parameters for the discussion. I would like to hand over to Harold Lind, who is going to talk about the case for advertising on the BBC.

Harold Lind: Thank you. You forgot to say what a sex symbol I am; I told you to put that in. Now let me make one point to start with. I am not in fact making a case for anything. I'm not saying what ought to happen to the BBC; I have no very keen interest one way or the other in what does happen to the BBC.

This is quite different from just about everybody else who has spoken, who obviously have very passionate interests in what happens to the BBC. As the poet Yeats put it so well, the best lack of conviction and the worst are full of passionate intensity – a point which came over in some of the earlier discussion.

What I am doing is putting forward a scenario, something which may well happen, and I'll give you my views for explaining why it may well happen and talk a little about the probability of it happening.

Why do I think that there is a very plausible scenario for saying that the BBC will be pushed towards taking television advertising? We had quite a lot yesterday about the possibilities of the BBC cutting its costs, but when you actually look at it a licence fee increase tied in with inflation from now on should really be enough for the BBC to manage properly. The quick answer to that is that in an ideal world that may well be true. Obviously there is a great deal of fat around the BBC bureaucracy and hierarchy which could be cut and if that was cut there might well be enough money to get by even when you increase the licence fee only at the rate of inflation. The reason why I say only is in fact that the cost of broadcasting is going up quite considerably above the rate of inflation.

Cresta said that she expected the BBC would have to cut its costs by 10% between now and 1996 to keep up with the licence fee. I think she is somewhat underestimating that; the real costs of running the BBC's present services with its present bureaucracy would actually go up considerably more above inflation than that. I would guess 20–30% but obviously we are talking pure guesswork here. Why don't I think that the BBC will be able to cut its bureaucracy and save money that way? The answer comes from another quotation, which goes "can the leopard change its spots or the bureaucrat his suit?" and the answer is that they never have in the past and I don't think they are going to do in any conceivable future either. Just like the Civil Service, they all make a lot of noise about it, redefine some people, fire a few tea ladies and re-hire them as freelances and say that they have cut their bureaucracy and aren't they good boys, and that would be very true, but it's not really going to do very much to help their costs.

The end result will be that by 1996 the BBC is going to be making very large squealing noises about just how poor it is and how much money it will need in any new review to get it back on any kind of reasonable level as it was in the good old days of whenever they consider the good old days to have been. They will do all the usual mobilising of all their squads of dancing bishops and worthy intellectuals and academics and so on to buttonhole everybody they can to explain why the BBC is so desperately poor and why something needs to be done about it. On the whole this has always worked pretty well in the past and it will probably continue to work pretty well in 1996, and will get over the people who matter that the BBC is jolly poor and something should be done about it. But the question is what.

Who will be the people who make the decisions in 1996? The essence is, that if it was Labour there would be no problems as far as the BBC was concerned; the Labour Party can always make sure that the poor can be induced to pay for the establishment to keep on doing what they are doing and I'm sure the BBC will find a way of raising the licence fee.

Let's just suppose that instead of Labour there is a Conservative government. The point I've made so far is that the BBC would at least say it was desperately short of money and almost certainly believe it was desperately short of money, and it would mobilize its squads to get this fact over. At the moment the politicians are squeezing round this lot by saying of course the BBC can make money by other methods, by for example some sort of minimal subscription, such as specialized subscription channels. Now that is one of the great non-starters of all time. BBC Select is a joke in slightly bad taste, but quite amusing just the same – it was tried with doctors who are the best commercial bet on this, and failed miserably. They are now talking about doing it for all sorts of strange groups, I think legal golfing Irishmen seem to be the people who are most at risk from BBC Select, and with all due respect to legal golfing Irishmen, I don't think they are going to make enough money to get the BBC out of the mess it would be in by 1996, and in fact if the BBC carries on with BBC Select I think it is going to cost money, rather than making money.

There was a suggestion yesterday that you could put the whole BBC service on subscription. That is actually a quite interesting method and would be a way of raising all the money the BBC wants, but we're talking about plausible scenarios and one certainty is that no government is going to do something which appears wildly unpopular as that; the $x\%$ of people who aren't going to pay the increased subscription fee would be screaming blue murder and possibly voting the wrong way. They still like *EastEnders* so no government is going to lose votes by doing anything at all like that. They are looking for a way of financing the BBC without losing votes.

The problem is that if they were simply going to raise the licence fee by the amount the BBC would need, if I'm right about their increasing costs, an increase of about 30 or 40% would be necessary to keep the BBC going for the next few years until the next licence review. Whatever anybody said yesterday about the fact that people really loved paying their licences, it isn't true. And no government believes it's true. We are talking about political realities and what governments are going to do to make sure they don't lose votes.

So the government finds itself in a cleft stick. Subscription revenue isn't going to work, large licence fee increases are going to be very unpopular, sponsorship will bring in a certain amount of money to help programmes to be made (but this is simply a way of getting programmes a bit more cheaply than they otherwise would be), and the final way of course would be subsidies from the taxpayer; but the last thing that

Conservatives, even wettish Conservatives, are likely to want to do is give subsidies from the taxpayer for the BBC.

So where does that leave your politician, your dryish Conservative politician, who has been told by the BBC that it is desperate for money and who believes the BBC is desperate for money? At that stage, if you're a politician, advertising may well look like a perfectly reasonable option on the grounds that most people don't really seem to mind very much having ads in the middle of their programmes. It isn't a disastrous option in the way that a very high licence fee increase, or universal subscription, would be. You would get your assorted bishops and the kind of people who are here screaming, but they aren't what you would call your overwhelming vote changers. Looked at from a Conservative government position in 1996, advertising might well look like the least bad option.

If it was the least bad option and they took it, what would then happen? Well various things would happen, but let me just make this simple point of what would happen to the Channel 3 contractors: it would be more or less totally disastrous. The share of advertising revenue going to ITV or Channel 3 was around 80% last year. If the BBC didn't take advertising this would fall to around 60% in the year 2000, with the new channels, Channel 4 and so taking the remainder. If the BBC *did* take advertising that 60% would fall to perhaps 35%. This would drive the Channel 3 contractors straight into the ground.

So what everybody has to do now is start working out a few probabilities: I've given you a scenario, I haven't said that that scenario will happen. I have just given you reasons for saying it is not a wildly implausible scenario. You could see events, circumstances, forcing certain people in that direction.

What are the probabilities, what are the odds? Obviously if there were a Labour government, you can give odds of 1000 to 1 against there being any advertising on the BBC. With a wettish Conservative government, greatly influenced by the dancing bishops, there would also probably no advertising on the BBC; with a dryish Conservative government, it would be much more likely – the sort of economic pressures I've talked about would make that kind of government at least think very carefully in that direction.

The Channel 3 contractors have to go along with their bids to the ITC perfectly happily grinning all over their faces and saying good heavens, no this absolutely couldn't happen. Quite manifestly, as I see it, it could happen, which leaves the Channel 3 contractors as they put in their bids with the thought that just possibly the BBC might take advertising in four or five years' time. Those among them who are old Etonians, might recognize this, which comes from Thomas Gray's *A Distant Prospect of Eton*, "alas regardless of their doom the little victims play, no sense of their wills to come nor cares beyond today". That does fit most of the people who work in television, and with this happy thought I will leave you.

Libby Child: Not surprisingly, in principle I am in favour of advertising on the BBC, given that I have worked in advertising for eleven years.

The case against advertising appearing on the BBC often hinges on two points of view, both of which I heard expressed yesterday afternoon:

33

(1) That advertising will be a pollutant, completely detrimental to viewers' enjoyment of BBC programmes; that it will somehow destroy the BBC's instrinsic and unique appeal to viewers; hardly a vote of confidence for the strength of the programmes.

(2) That pressure from advertisers for maximum ratings will lead to "lowest common denominator programming" so that the minute paid-for advertising appears the BBC schedule will be unrecognisable.

I do not accept either of these points.

Let's begin by looking at it from a consumer's point of view.

£77 may indeed represent value for money, and not seem like a great deal to those of us who have spent more just getting up here and back, but for many people it still represents a significant outlay.

It is twice what the average family spends on a child's clothes in a year, more than they spend on electricity in a quarter. It could keep them in loo rolls for over three years. Why, when there are alternative options, should we be asked to pay this sum for half our television service, and a portion of our radio?

A recent survey concluded that more people would rather see advertising on the BBC than continue to pay a licence fee. Amongst heavy TV viewers, 70% would rather have advertising on the BBC than continue to pay a licence fee. This did not take account of the fact that the advertising could be controlled, by limiting the number of minutes of advertising appearing in one hour and keeping some advertising between rather than during programmes. One can only assume that if these options had been given, the response would have been even more in favour of advertising appearing on the BBC.

This comes as no surprise to people working in the advertising industry, who realize that advertising, far from being an irritant, is actively enjoyed by many viewers.

A recent survey conducted by London Weekend Television asked children what they enjoyed watching on TV. Top of the charts was the advertising, with 87% saying that they enjoyed watching commercials, with the nearest programme, *Neighbours*, achieving a 70% vote. The most popular programme specifically designed for children was *Grange Hill*, which came in at number 7 with a 60% rating. Interestingly, both those programmes are on the BBC, so from that one could conclude that the kids wouldn't mind if they saw ads during their well-liked programmes.

But nor would their Mums and Dads. In 1988 81% of the population claimed to approve of advertising a little or a lot. This figure has increased considerably over the last twenty years. Only 13% actively disapproved of advertising. In 1961 it was nearer 50%.

The reason for this, I believe, is that the nature of advertising has changed dramatically over that time. We are now producing commercials which people really enjoy watching, with few exceptions.

From a viewer's perspective advertising is already appearing on the BBC. We've been deluged by Floyd and Gloria Hunniford advertising the *Radio Times*. Whilst the

34

Saddler inquiry might throw its hands up in horror, I'm sure it passes without much comment in the average household. After all, it is indistinguishable from what they see on ITV.

But it can hardly pass without comment from an advertiser. It is hypocritical to argue against ads and then do this.

Planning for BBC Enterprises assumes a high level of on-air promotion. Strange practice indeed from a company which believes advertisers are tainted beings.

It is touted that should paid-for advertising ever appear on the BBC, the schedule would change beyond recognition, as these nasty commercial animals – advertisers – sought high-rating low quality mindless pap. This is the last thing advertisers want.

Increasingly, advertisers have very specifically targeted messages. The days of mass market blanket advertising, whilst not over, are certainly numbered. This is driven not just by the fragmentation of media that we are seeing currently, but also by advertisers' own desire to reach the people they actually want and not waste time and money talking to those who they don't. The BBC would therefore be a valuable addition to many advertisers' schedules. It would give us a great opportunity to reach a more upmarket audience, one that watches less television for example.

This works in the Press, with national newspapers and magazines. Some of the newspapers with lowest circulation have the highest cost per thousand, for example the *Financial Times*. Because they are offering a very specific type of audience, one not easily available.

It is also very wrong to pretend that the BBC does not chase volume ratings with *Neighbours*, *EastEnders*, and *Only Fools and Horses*. It is grossly hypocritical for them to pretend that this is not one of their corporate aims and objectives.

So I believe advertising on the BBC would be welcomed by viewers and would not, in itself, cause a change in the structure of the schedule. But in practice, it can't happen within the next 12 years thanks to the government's lack of foresight. At the moment the ITV companies are busy preparing their franchise applications, projecting advertising revenue for the next 10 years. If this government allows advertising on the BBC to appear in 1996, under a different charter, this of course would completely skew the ITV companies' predictions, and could potentially cause many to go out of business. Clearly this would be extremely bad news for advertisers and for viewers who could see ITV competition merging on the programme guidelines set down in the franchise applications.

But in principle, advertising on the BBC remains desirable. Viewers would rather see the advertising on the BBC than continue to pay the licence fee.

Gillian Laidlaw: You may have noticed that different organizations which you have known – either as an employee, a visitor, a supplier or a customer – have a different "feel" to them. Different things are important: people "get on better" or "fit in better" in some organizations than others; different types of behaviour are expected or encouraged; people value or have pride in different things. Together these things contribute to what is described as the culture of an organization, and although that is fast becoming an over-used word it is an issue in which everyone is taking an interest nowadays.

So here is one way of defining the culture of an organization: the shared beliefs, values and patterns of behaviour which lie behind what the organization rewards, supports and expects.

When I was asked to talk about how the culture of the BBC will change if it has to take advertising I decided to talk to people who have worked in organizations which have taken advertising for years, namely some of the independent television companies. I also talked to people who work with the BBC. I asked them questions like – "what do people here believe in?" "who gets on around here?" "what kinds of behaviour and skills get rewarded – not just in financial terms abut who gets recognized, praised, promoted?"

And I got some remarkably similar answers. The conclusion I had to draw was that the culture of both the BBC and ITV, especially at programme-making level, is at present very similar. People who had worked for both agreed with me. Yet ITV companies have been taking advertising since 1955. So it seems unlikely that simply taking advertising will require the BBC to change its culture.

The real issue is how the new source of income is treated within the BBC, for example whether it has a direct impact at the level of individual programme making or whether it is simply added to the total funds available to run the organization.

So I then explored how changes in income can affect the culture of an organization. My firm has considerable experience of working with public sector organizations who have had to cope with revised sources of government funding. This has usually meant that they can no longer rely on regular government handouts, that they have had to compete for business in the marketplace and survival depends on their ability to offer excellent products and services priced competitively with private sector organizations. Such companies have hitherto been sheltered from competitive forces. They have grown fat and bureaucratic. They have administrators not managers. Decision is by committee. They have procedures and rule books but lack the basic cost information and control and management information systems which private sector organizations found essential years ago. Furthermore they often believe that they know better than their customers what their customers want and competition, when it comes, is a rude shock.

This description sounds suspiciously like the BBC and quite a few of the independent television companies.

We all know that many of the independent television companies have made dramatic changes recently to create leaner, fitter organizations to compete for their franchises. Such changes have been necessary for their survival and these changes will, in due course, affect their culture. Most significant will be when budgeting and individual performance play an increasingly significant role in the organization, when individuals are rewarded for their performance against predefined targets and when people at all levels in the organization believe that hitting those targets really matters.

This is the kind of thing which Kinsley Lord has helped public sector organizations to do as well. A common theme in our work has been to raise the awareness of the need to respond to customer demands and hence to reduce internal bureaucracy, to increase personal accountability, to improve internal information and support systems and to make a direct link for the first time between profitability and customer satisfaction. Such dramatic changes result in new beliefs, values and patterns of behaviour – in short, the culture of the organization changes.

But changing culture is difficult, threatening and uncomfortable. It does not happen because the boss says it will be so. It happens when people throughout an organization understand that there will be benefits if they begin to behave differently. In our experience a major external shock is usually necessary before the need to change is recognized. Those could be shocks like the competition faced by BT since it has been privatized, the rapid increases in oil prices in the 1970s which meant that oil companies had to rethink their strategies, changes in interest rates which attracted the high street banks into mortgage lending thus attacking the market which had traditionally belonged to building societies, or the shock now faced by the independent television companies, the requirement to repitch for their franchises.

So why should the BBC change? Does it need to change? Can you treat programmes in the same way as you can gas or electricity?

First of all the BBC has got to make some decisions about the kind of role it wishes to play in British broadcasting.

Taking advertising, adding funds from a new source to the pot, will not of itself mean that the BBC has to start doing things differently. Our experience says that something more fundamental has to kickstart the process. Perhaps it will be exposure to the realities of true competition or perhaps it will be the renegotiation of its charter and licence agreement. Yes, I believe a culture change is necessary, but a major external shock is required which will prompt the BBC to take the actions that will change its behaviour and hence its culture.

Richard Wade: I promise I didn't know what Gillian was going to say, because I may go on from where she began. But can I make one thing absolutely crystal clear to start with? I'm not going to speak on behalf of the Advertising Association for the simple reason that the Advertising Association is in fact a conglomerate at the centre of 30 other associations which represent all the different interests in advertising, including advertisers, agencies and media, so there are radically differing views on whether it would be a good thing or not if the BBC took advertising.

I'm going to speak quite separately and I shan't either give my own views, but one or two of the scenarios that Gillian and Harold have floated may come up in what I've got to say. I'm simply going to try and capture what may be future echoes of what I expect other people to say over the next few years, as a decision is taken on the future of the BBC. Some people believe that there will be a major and radical change in the shape size and funding, but I must admit to being a dyed-in-the- wool BBC man; well I was – now I'm probably just a greying sheep in wolf's clothing.

The total UK advertising market is about £8 billion a year. The licence fee income of the BBC is £1.2 billion. You could not open the whole of the BBC to unrestricted advertising without turning the media in this country upside down, and in doing so undermining commercial television and damaging some sectors of radio and press.

Other speakers have made that clear; it is absolutely not an option that I have heard from any thinking strategist.

Other speakers of course have already made the point that the BBC does already advertise, and the Saddler committee has suggested that it should avoid what some felt to be unfair competition in the magazine market.

Now if the BBC does already advertise, what about partial advertising or subscription or sponsorship? Many people – more people that the BBC would like to admit – believe that a compulsory licence fee could be a dead duck in 1996. Harold Lind raised the question as to whether subscription was a possibility; if you describe subscription as a voluntary licence fee then it has greater credibility.

Originally the BBC was the national instrument of broadcasting; you remember the Home, Light and Third programmes, the young BBC Television from Alexandra Palace, plus of course the unique and still peerless overseas service. Then came BBC 2 in 1964, a complementary service of culture and ideas and that made it an even stronger national broadcasting corporation. Later that empire grew and changed with pop radio, local radio, breakfast TV and eventually day-time television. The BBC became all-embracing. It competed on every front. The colour TV licences had given us a constantly increasing income. Some seemed to feel we were invincible. Then the ethos began to change as competition raised its head.

So we started to compete flat out for audience. Keep half the audience or we lose the licence fee – that is what they were saying. I know, I was there. First BBC 2 became the snooker channel and we were entranced by the audience figures. Local radio, which started as a pure community service, turned increasingly to pop, quite under-standable. The original breakfast television was everything that a folksy American network could wish and excellent of its kind. We became sort of commercial broad-casters except that we had a guaranteed income. Other subtle and powerful changes of culture were at work too. Co-production, the injection of substantial non-BBC monies into individual series gently changed some of our attitudes towards editorial control. The advent of sponsorship increased this tendency. We had first the external dynamic of sponsored events like Embassy snooker and, more recently, the active pursuit of sponsorship to support major events like the Proms.

The former BBC Chairman, Stuart Young, who approached broadcasting like the able accountant he was, was right about one thing when talking about commercial funding – you can't be a little bit pregnant. But if the BBC has become pregnant, and that's obviously a matter of discussion, what's it going to do about it?

I really don't know. I have been outside the BBC for five years. But one possible answer you may hear is for mixed funding – part commercial with advertising and part licence fee and/or part subscription to encode its signals – because, as I say, you could sell subscription as a voluntary licence fee.

But why? Well if, say, you were a visitor from Papua New Guinea, coming into this country for the first time and you just looked at the broadcasting that's on offer, what would you regard as "commercial"? Well, it might be ITV, BBC 1, BBC 2, BSkyB, cable, with independent radio, Radio 1, Radio 2 and some of local radio. That you might regard, if you just looked or listened, as commercial. But what would our Papuan friend regard as public service in the classical sense of cultural resources? It might be Channel 4, Radio 3, Radio 4, Jazz FM, ethnic radio, I don't know – a different kind of group. I'll leave Radio 5 and purely regional services out of this skeletal argument if I may.

But that very crude notional split between those which are commercially fundable and those which are culturally important simply doesn't work because already you've got a mixture – Channel 4, for example, is commercial in any case.

So what might you see post-1996 if we were in for a radical change? Or rather what might you see if the BBC wanted to try and win the battle for the licence fee or a subscription charge? What could it do to provide a service that most viewers would agree that they wanted and would be prepared to pay for on a voluntary basis?

Let's take an extreme scenario. If you take radio, you might hear a proposal something like this – it's the kind of equation that some people were playing with at the time of Peacock. Privatize Radios 1 and 2 with advertising but without cutting the ground from under existing commercial services. The BBC could become a provider of ethnic documentary, drama, consumer programmes to all channels, radio and television, as well as doing their own programmes. You might then get leaner and slimmer Radios 3 and 4 cross-funded either by a general TV licence or a TV subscription fee. It is not possible to fund Radios 3 and 4 by radio only licence or subscription. They are jewels in the BBC's crown and they must be protected and without them there would be no BBC as we now know it and understand it.

For television, you might hear people putting forward an argument that said something like this: privatize one channel with advertising, the market might be able to stand that without catastrophic effects on other channels throughout the media. Converge the remaining BBC output onto a single BBC television channel with those elements of excellence – drama, documentaries, events, sport, comedy – on which the Corporation has built its reputation, plus, of course, news and current affairs. This could be a relatively high price subscription channel without advertising.

Surgery – yes; radical – yes, very. But these are the kind of arguments I would expect some people to be putting forward in the next two or three years.

I have only briefly mentioned sponsorship. If advertising is alleged to alter editorial perception (though I don't, by the way, think that the Independent newspaper sways in the advertisers' wind particularly, do you?) then what does sponsorship do? It is small beer at the moment – say only £200 million a year. But some producer friends tell me that it does alter their editorial approach. So you might see increasing resistance from some programme makers. On the other hand I suspect that sponsorship will increase and be a useful outlet for some advertisers but never, I suspect, a major force in British broadcasting.

So there will be some voices saying that advertising on the BBC is inevitable. But it is not for those parts of the traditional BBC that other forms of funding can reach. If those sections that are already, on this argument, commercial are privatized then there is a bright new market for advertisers on ex-BBC channels and services. And within a new slim-line BBC? Well, a small robust core of excellence with one twenty-four hour television channel for time-shifted and live viewers plus Radios 3 and 4 and a production house in both television and radio producing and selling those programmes few other institutions are likely to produce extensively in the late 1990s: ethnic, consumer, documentary, classic drama and so on.

Why should the BBC be faced with such sweeping change? At the moment ITV is faced with a landscape even more traumatic. They are faced with the extinction of their franchises. So it would surprise some outsiders if the BBC did not at least have to consider very radical change. The advertising and licence fee based duopoly has produced broadcasting in Britain that is unique in the world. The ethos of the BBC has already changed. It might be able to cope with the cultural change that some commercial funding would bring. It could even cope, I suspect, with a careful movement to part privatization or loss of some existing activities. Those are not options I personally would bid for because I think there is, if the BBC wants to avoid that kind of radical proposition, quite a different scenario and one which other media certainly might welcome, though possibly not advertisers. And it's very simple – it's simply to convince the whole of the British public that at 21 pence a day the licence fee is the best value that anybody could possibly imagine, but they would have to start tomorrow and not in 1994.

One thing I am told loud and clear by friends in Government and ex-colleagues is that if the BBC you know and love is to survive then it must be braver and more radical in re-organization than ever before.

But, finally, let me speak for myself. I have a profound admiration for independent television and commercial radio. They provide many magnificent services. Channel 4 was a splendid innovation. And the BBC, as far as I'm concerned, is one of the world's great cultural institutions of all time and I wish it well.

. . .

During the discussion, the following were among the points made:

One speaker made the point that the Broadcasting Research Unit spent 18 months looking at different systems of broadcasting funding throughout the world. There was mixed funding in New Zealand, in Ireland, in Canada, in Germany, and it did not work the pressure was always on for managers and politicians to increase the commercial element.

To this Harold Lind responded that he had been waiting for someone to make that point for some time. What, he asked, was meant by the word "work"? What the speaker was saying was that the system of mixed funding didn't work in other countries. Was that to mean that whatever system we had worked here? The system we had here, he said, clearly worked in the interests of the programme makers, and particularly the people who run the BBC: someone provided them with money and they used that money for the purposes that they thought best. Did anybody else particularly believe in this, other than the programme makers?

One speaker from the floor made the point that the quality of the output of most of the ITV companies managed to stay the same. They had not been tainted in the way some seemed to suggest, by advertising. It might be argued in response that that was because they had the challenge of the BBC shining as a guiding light. The speaker thought that the ITV companies were are more responsible than that.

A further speaker thought that a way to change the culture of the BBC would be in the appointment of the Chairman and of the governors. She suggested someone like Anita Roddick of Body Shop as Chair, and as governors women who could actually stand and be successful in industry.

A representative of the advertising sector noted that the view of the advertisers had changed. If ITV held its audience, or if the fragmentation works, and if the audience for commercial television stays about 50%, there would not be an enormous pressure from advertisers for more time. But if didn't, and if the audience for commercial television got down to about 20% or 30%, and the BBC still held 50% of the audience, then the pressure would be enormous to put advertising on the BBC.

An independent consultant endorsed the view that the BBC taking advertising would itself not have any effect on the culture of the BBC. People making programmes looked for high ratings because they enjoyed the fact that a lot of people have appreciated their product. The argument against advertising on the BBC had nothing to do with tainting the BBC; it was really about the funding argument, the scarcity of advertising revenue, and the effect it would have on ITV. The advertising industry's motive in this was to get advertising at the lowest possible cost to it. The speaker argued that the advertising industry had shot itself in the foot because by arguing for more services to create more competition, it is, in fact fragmenting the audience that it previously could buy in a single buy through ITV. It would ideally have liked two ITVs, both of them with exactly the same audience profile as ITV 1. Mathematically that was not not possible. But the point was that if the BBC took two minutes of advertising and was charging x, the advertising industry would be up in arms and say that the BBC was artificially restricting supply and would demand that they take three minutes or four minutes so that they could halve the costs with the same revenue.

A representative of the BBC noted that it had been suggested that if the Corporation were to start a campaign of persuasion for the licence fee it would have to begin tomorrow and not in 1995. Would that be practical and was the time right? There would be no point in doing it if it were actually a scheme that was on its way out and it were just a question of how fast it died. It would be necessary to look and see whether it was a realistic possibility. Pluralism would bring new forms of funding. Instead of comparing the cost of the licence fee with that of ITV, which is seen to be free, people would compare it with the very high prices of subscription television. These things would count in the licence fee's favour.

However, Harold Lind on the platform argued against what he saw as an optimistic view about the way the BBC's finances will look in 1996. He added: "What one should really talk about is the way the advertisers are going to look at advertising in the BBC, and the idea that you suddenly get a large number of new advertising television sources coming in so the BBC becomes less relevant. There has actually been no shortage of advertising time for advertisers for at least the last seven, eight or 10 years. The amount of time – that is minutes of advertising for advertisers – has about trebled in the last 10 years. And that is far faster than any increase in advertising. It's trebled in the sense that Channel 4 has created an increase of about 50% or 60% in minuteage. They have very much longer broadcasting hours, after midnight till one, two, or three a.m. The minutes have increased, but the advertisers will not invest because the audience isn't increased. What the advertisers have always been short of is mass audiences for peak time and that didn't increase. And the advertisers want a mass audience for advertising. BBC 1 looks as good as it ever did and unless the BBC collapses in its audience over the next few years the advertisers, to get that mass audience, will still need BBC 1."

Another speaker addressed the issue of niche advertising. A great deal of niche advertising space was already available. If an advertiser wanted any particular minority, the odds were it could be found. It would probably be on Channel 4 and it would probably be after 10.30 in the evening or in the afternoon. There was no great shortage of them. The shortage was for those advertisers who wanted "coverage" – who wanted to get a large number of people watching their advertisements. It was not the same as mass advertising, but it was close.

A representative of Channel 4 remarked that the lobby for advertising on the BBC deserved congratulation. Its case had been killed completely stone dead at least three times and here it was all over again. The strongest argument was that if you put advertising on the BBC you destroyed the system. Presumably the point of a policy of funding broadcasting was to make broadcasting better – that was to say to improve the quality of programmes and increase the range of programme choices available to viewers. If there were advertising on the BBC and it destroyed the rest of the system, these things could not possibly be achieved. This should have really put an end to the argument. The question about what advertising did to programmes was about the relationship between the sources of funding of broadcasting and the sort of broadcasting that generally resulted. Advertisers bought time on television because they wanted to sell products to viewers. There was nothing wrong with that, but it produced a certain kind of television, very broadly speaking. The argument for a licence fee was that somewhere in the national system it gave a place where people made decisions about broadcasting only motivated by professional judgement about what would amuse or interest audiences. The problem of accountability of the BBC for its decisions was a serious problem, because if the market gave no clear demonstration then how could accountability be achieved? The politicians wanted it to be directly answerable to them but that created other problems. We had not solved the problem of accountability and it had to be addressed before the licence fee argument would really go away.

Another speaker suggested that most of those in the room were broadcasters and that they were looking at matters from a broadcaster's point of view. The future of the BBC was a political decision and it was the politicians who would make it. Despite the best efforts even of the Tories the amount of taxation, both direct and indirect, that they could take from the population was decreasing. It had now reached its maximum and they had to reduce it. That was why the licence fee was under threat. He went on to suggest that the way around this problem was to privatize the BBC. We needed to sell it off because we needed to renew the whole process of public service broadcasting. One reason was that the BBC represented the Establishment, embodying those modest, benign, patrician attitudes that kept this society stuck where it was, in a backwater of faded glory. Public broadcasting was really important but the BBC was not the one structure any more. The answer was to create new structures and that meant actually getting rid of the BBC.

Those who contributed to the discussion included:

Liz Ashton-Hill, BBC Select
Steven Barnett, Henley Centre
Jim Brown, consultant
Andrew Curry, independent producer
John Fearn, BBC Regional Advisory Council
Liz Forgan, Channel 4
James Gordon, Radio Clyde
David Hallan, Community Service Volunteers
Barbara Hosking, Yorkshire Television
Peter Marr, Incorporated Society of British Advertisers
Hannah Pout, Bar Ilan University
David Rushton, Institute of Local Television
Michael Starks, BBC

4 Whose hands on the button?

John Forrest
National Transcommunications Ltd

Bryce McCrirrick
Consultant

Stephen Temple
Department of Trade and Industry

George Cook
Consultant, Quantel

Chair: Colin Shaw
Director, Broadcasting Standards Council

Colin Shaw: It seemed to me and to other people on the Steering Committee to be something of an anomaly that at a conference which was concerned with broadcasting there had been for quite a long time no regular sessions taken up with engineering issues, and for too long it seemed to me that one half of the two cultures had ruled out discussion of the other. The Symposium has in recent years been much absorbed with talk of money and markets and that is partly because they represent new elements in British broadcasting. They have of course been prominent in debates and discussions on broadcasting in other parts of the world but they are, in a sense, new phenomena in this part of the world.

But you don't need to think very long about the history of broadcasting to understand how influential engineering considerations have been in determining the course of that history. We meet today in Manchester, the headquarters since the 1920s of the BBC Regional Broadcasting Committee, functioning for most of the time within England, inside regions whose size and shape were dictated by the engineering possibilities. It was engineering considerations again, a little qualified by consider-ations of advertising revenue, which dictated the shape of the original independent television franchise areas more than 35 years ago.

In terms of technical innovation, however, it was usually the broadcasters who called the shots, and who, in a limited British market, decided which technical projects would prosper and which would not. It was the broadcasters who made the running for the consumer, not always very successfully as the long climb to the ascendancy of FM listening was to prove but in general, just as what was good for General Motors

44

in the United States was thought good, at least by General Motors, for America in general, so what was good for the British broadcasters in their view at least tended to be pretty good for the British manufacturer and probably not so terrible for the British consumer.

But the position is changing. John Forrest, whom we are delighted to have with us this morning sits on the platform as Chairman of National Transcommunications, the newly liberated engineering division of the old Independent Broadcasting Authority. There used to be, in the IBA, an engineer called Bob Cameron; he was the IBA's engineer in Northern Ireland, and he always referred to those of us who worked in the IBA at Brompton Road as "the political wing of the IBA". I'm not quite sure what that makes John at National Transcommunications, but I think there was a kind of message for us there somewhere. Bryce McCrirrick is now a consultant; he was formerly the BBC's Director of Engineering and in the next few years he may have to contemplate a BBC engineering division free to compete with Transcom and who knows what other organizations. What has happened to Transcom, and might happen to the BBC's engineering division, raises questions about the future of research and design in this country. And that's something which is certainly a matter of concern to the Department of Trade and Industry and we are especially glad to see Stephen Temple here as a symbol, a harbinger perhaps, of a greater willingness on the part of at least one Whitehall giant to debate these issues in public. He comes from the DTI, whose interests, he tells me, lie not so much in promoting the welfare of British industry as in creating the climate in which the welfare of British industry can then look after itself.

And in the fourth member of the panel, George Cook, we have a former senior BBC engineer who joined up with Quantel, a manufacturer who in making technical innovations has forged perhaps unique links with producers and directors. Two substantial sectors of interest have escaped the net this morning and we should perhaps record their absences. First the politicians who are obliged to take the crucial decisions on the nation's behalf, and the audience – the consumers – who will have to put up with the consequences of the decisions taken by the politicians and indeed by the former members of the panel and their colleagues at home and abroad.

I thought we might begin this morning by looking at one particular corner of the battlefield – the battle for high-definition television. High-definition television seems to me to have been with us for a long time. It seems, and indeed is, many years since I watched the first demonstration of its special magic. I have seen it many times since but if I never see another bird flicking off the water drops in a bird-bath it will not be too soon.

High-definition television brings us into touch with the MAC family – C-MAC, D-MAC, and the rest, and I wanted to begin by asking John Forrest to tell us where we now stand and then invite the other panel members to make their contribution. We are going to try and make it a conversation between the panel and the floor.

John Forrest: HDTV is indeed a very interesting problem to start with because it is quite specific and may be rather futuristic, but I think it will bring up quite a few of the points that are very important to this debate about whose hands are on the button. Since we have been told not to get into technical details to a great extent, certainly not

45

for a start, I thought it might be useful just to review very quickly the background to HDTV for those who are not familiar with it and the very complex debate that has gone on for the last couple of years. I think it is important to identify first the need for the market and indeed whether there is a market. Television engineers are always striving to try to match the quality that has been portrayed in the cinema and I use the term "television engineers" very deliberately because I think that says something about the approach which has been very much technology-led. It has been the engineers and the technologists who have been striving over the years to bring these new innovations forward. We have not seen thousands of people congregating on Downing Street saying "We must have HDTV". We didn't see that with colour television. Something better than we have now obviously has to come in terms of television; I think it is an inevitability that the technology will deliver a product which viewers in general feel will give some extra quality.

The real attraction probably is its larger screens. It is really the very fact of having a larger screen that leads one to the need for higher definition because quite honestly the definition really is about good enough on the normal-sized screen in most people's home. The aspect ratio of wider screens is felt to be an attraction, more akin to the famous golden mean of the artists, with its slightly wider picture and of course its compatibility with the cinema and the film medium.

The problem that technologists have always had has been how to introduce innovations. The significant part about our business, in terms of transmission and getting the signal to viewers, is that the dominant part of the investment lies in the hands of the viewers in their homes. If you take the U.K. for example, there is about £10 billion worth of investment in equipment in people's homes. That dwarfs the investment in the transmission infrastructure and indeed in equipment in the programme companies. So there is always a problem of how you bring in these new innovations when you've got these sets sitting in people's homes. The introduction of colour and more recently of NICAM stereo sound had to be done in a way that would not disadvantage the existing viewers. At least that's always been the thinking in Europe. Of course it could be argued that the easiest way to do it is to introduce it in a non-compatible way. So you've got the two approaches; you can try and fit it in to the existing structure somehow so you don't disadvantage viewers or else you say this is something new, it's very special, I'm afraid we're only going to keep the old system going for a certain time, you've got to buy all new equipment.

In HDTV the Japanese over ten years ago decided that this was the way of the future and they decided to tackle a non-compatible system, something that would be totally new, delivered on a different means – via satellite – and would not use the existing equipment. This brings me to certain rather important aspects of technology and markets. The Japanese were prepared to fund and to countenance a very long period of losses or at least capital investment with very little return in order to get that new system into the marketplace. That could be done in their kind of economic structure. The broadcaster, NHK, was prepared to bear those tremendous costs in that very long period of slow build-up of sets as the new system came into being.

Europe chose the compatible route with a low-cost entry, the idea being that one should introduce something that was low-cost to the viewer to start with and then build on it and gradually evolve over with steady improvements through enhanced definition to high definition. That is very much hinged on the much more short-term structures in Europe associated with funding of business; these structures are very much dependent on rapid return on investment and it is difficult to countenance now, I think, any non-compatible entry of such systems in the European environment.

Where do we stand? That was the question that has been a standards battle which we have all heard about. Many people have felt it somewhat ideological that the standards battle has been very much related to penetration of Japanese products and Japanese industry into the European environment but I think as much as anything it is related to the market structures. In Japan this noncompatible introduction was much more viable. I've mentioned one reason but there is also the fact that they have great difficulty in getting television to their islands and therefore a new system could provide initially quite a strong marketplace.

In Europe we went for the compatible introduction of HDTV via direct broadcast satellite and we've seen of late the difficulties that have occurred as result of a market force approach becoming very much stronger and starting to destroy strategies that were based very much on the past on technology-led approaches driven by major organizations. And I ought to mention the U.S. because there are three legs to this tripod and HDTV satellite delivery has not so far been shown really to be a viable proposition for the majority of homes. The drive really comes from the terrestrial networks, the big network providers who are losing market share and need something to deliver a new product and therefore the drive in the U.S. has been very much towards a delivery system which is terrestrially rather than satellite based.

My view is that it's not so much ideologies but markets now which are very much driving these things.

The question in this session is where are we, whose hand is on the button? That is becoming very much less clear. Until relatively recently it was clearly the broadcasters, because the broadcasters and their various organizations did the research and development. In essence then they went to industry having agreed between themselves about standardization and told industry to manufacture the products. We now see industry taking a very much stronger lead in this whole process and driving the market so we move from a technology-led environment to a market-driven approach; and then you have to answer the question, is there a real market approach to HDTV? I would guess that the answer to that, at present, is that it is somewhat doubtful, which means that in terms of HDTV it is going to be rather slow entering the market place and particularly slow in market driven economies in Europe, and particularly in the U.K., where we have largely abandoned technology-led approaches to very short-term market-driven approaches.

The Japanese will undoubtedly continue and we see there a very interesting aspect too in this process of trying to determine whose hand is on the button – a desire to bring the programme material under the control of the equipment manufacturer under a common umbrella so as to establish a means of driving the product into the market place – the acquisition of Columbia Pictures, for example, and MCA recently by Japanese industry is a crucial factor in this process.

Now we are seeing in many of these technological innovations that it is the industry that has its hand on the button, that the broadcasters' hands have been moved away from the button. However, it's not quite as simple as that because there is no use in having a product in the market place if there are no programmes. We all agree that what is required to get the product accepted is programmes, so the industry is going to have to recruit the broadcasters to help it press that button.

Stephen Temple: When I saw the title of this session, what it invoked in my mind was who within the broadcasting organizations is driving the innovation? Is it the technical side putting before the production side all the technical possibilities in saying "look this is new, whether you like it or not this is the way we should be going", or is it the production side saying "this is what we need, never mind whether it is feasible, give it to me and I want it today"? Who within the broadcasting organizations is the driving force for innovation? I think what I am going to argue this morning is that if you are not careful the answer will be none of you. The finger on the button will be that of an alliance of manufacturing interests and civil servants in Brussels.

Now as you know, buttons come in two colours; there is a green button and a red button, so that if this alliance develops and gets political ascendancy in Brussels it will be their finger that says this technology will go and this will not go. There is also a stop button; you can conceive of regulations that say your screens will be blacked out on this technology because it is not the preferred technology. We want to try to create a market environment where the user has a choice – Henry Ford, I think, was the analogy: any colour as long as it's black. That is really the scenario I can set before you and you may say it is a bit far-fetched.

Well, let's see if it is so far-fetched. Let's pull the curtain back and look at the discussions that are actually going on last week and this week in Brussels in terms of what is called the MAC directive. This was a directive that was produced in 1986, and it was brought in in a little bit of a rush – if I recall – because the Italians were thought to be a little bit wobbly on MAC and therefore we had to get something in pretty quickly. At least that was what we were told – I'm sure the Italians were told it was the British who were a bit wobbly but, whoever was saying what to whom, a directive was tabled by the Commission. What this directive said is that on a certain range of frequency channels which were internationally then recognized as the frequency channels for direct-to-home broadcasting, only the MAC family of standards would be used. That was a variation on a nice old dispute within Europe in terms of the family because there were lots of different versions of MAC but that is another story. Let's call it the MAC family, and this was brought in on the books and I think the U.K. had already committed itself anyway on that range of frequencies to the MAC standard and those frequency channels were advertised on the basis that if you wanted to use those frequency channels it's the MAC standards you have to use. Now, to a certain extent that sounds a little bit interventionist but on the other hand it had a high degree of market-driven element because no one was obliged to come forward in that competition, so everyone had a free choice whether they wanted to bid or not. But if they bid then the rules of the competition were that they came forward on the MAC standard.

Now there was another range of frequencies that were recognized internationally for long-distance, transatlantic or intercontinental communications, for telecommunication purposes. Part of telecommunications – under the old monopoly arrangements – was the conveying of television broadcasting programmes from one continent to another, not to the general public but between the broadcasting organizations. Due to some pretty clever advances in technology the sort of dishes you need shrunk from those 97 ft dishes you see down in Goonhilly in Cornwall down to about 10 ft in the early seventies and by the mid to late seventies it had got down to one or two metres, and if you stripped out the rain margins – you know, so that when it rains you weren't too fussed that there was a little bit of noise on the picture – you could get it down to about a metre in diameter. That opened up a way round the MAC directive which Sky, as you know, was not slow in spotting, and via the Astra satellite Sky brought in a broadcasting service that circumvented the MAC directive.

As a net result of that, within the U.K. environment, we had this competition between Sky and BSB, which was a competition not just for programmes, but also for technology because if you bought one kind of receiver you were locked out of the other, for no other reason than the different technical standards, apart from the fact you had to point your dishes to different positions in the sky.

One of the problems of new technology is that things sometimes don't go according to grand plans and grand strategies. The MAC decoding equipment was late arriving in the market place and that delayed BSB and so you've read in your newspapers that there's been this merger.

To bring you up-to-date, the directive actually expires at the end of this year so that at the end of this year if the civil servants in Brussels, who have the unique ability to put proposals for Ministers, do nothing then it would just be a free-for-all and those who have invested in MAC would see their prospects and chances being reduced.

So they are bending the Commission's ears back, saying "this is terrible, this Sky route around the directive was almost tantamount to a fiddle – what we want is a directive that will catch everything". So these two ranges of frequencies – the ones that were intended for direct-to-home and the ones that were intended for telecommunications – all of them – should be subject to a requirement to use MAC where the intention is to broadcast to the members of the general public. And by the way, they want it to be retrospective. They want the screen switched off for PAL, so that all those million and a quarter Astra viewers will immediately become a market for MAC receivers which are at the moment in their warehouses – and they've got rather a lot of them.

So that is one faction in Brussels which is bending the Commission's ears back. Now there are more more moderate voices and, here, I'm given to understand the French are prepared to be quite reasonable. They are saying they would accept a two-year transition period and then black out the PAL screens. The Germans, who have been our allies in telecommunications liberalization, have been even more liberal because they're prepared to see simulcasting. They say you're allowed to broadcast in PAL but you are forced also to broadcast in MAC. So that is their particular approach and within Germany they have got a Memorandum of Understanding which encompasses this principle which sounds a bit draconian but they are even more liberal because they are prepared to subsidize out of public expense the broadcasters who go in for the simulcasting – that's the particular way the Germans are viewing life.

What is the U.K. view on this? Well as you know Whitehall has this great propensity for open government and in pursuit of this I am about to reveal to you exactly what our position is and in the spirit of that I would draw your attention to the Official Secrets Act; should you reveal anything I am about to tell you I am sure there is a section somewhere that will cover this. Our position is that we feel that first of all the MAC argument is rather a narrow vision of the future because satellite viewers are only a small percentage of the whole. I imagine probably 3–5% would be rather an optimistic figure. So what about all the terrestrial viewers – are they never going to get better pictures? There is research going on in Germany, which the BBC has joined – an international research consortium – on trying to improve PAL pictures, PAL Plus I think is the name it goes under. But essentially they want to strap two side panels on the side of your picture so that you too as terrestrial viewers might be able to see the sort of thing that comes out of the cinema industry.

What about a global standard? John hinted about the battle two or three years ago for the MAC standard where it's pretty clear that MAC could never really form the basis of a global standard. I don't think the Americans or the Japanese will go down that road. So if you believe in global standards, and our Government is committed to an open global trading system and competition on a global basis, what about a global transmission system? One of those golden rules in standardization is that if you're in a real mess, don't frig around with the present mess, leap over it and look for the next technology breakpoints. Go sufficiently far into the future where people's pockets are not touched and then try to start getting people together to bring together some sort of global transmission standard.

I'm told by the experts that point in the far future is digital. That would be the way to go – not MAC, but a digital HDTV standard. Our particular view on life is to give MAC its chance – we're quite prepared to see a renewal directive that will put frequencies and orbit slots to one side for the MAC standard – but we are not for saying exclusively that is the only route, and we would like to see the possibility of terrestrial viewers having their chance for better pictures. We would like to see the big research people start to lay the foundation for that long-term global standard, and meanwhile MAC can have its go in the market place as the thing will bring wide screens into the home in the next two or three years, or even sooner. We are also completely against any cut-off date for PAL. It seems to us to be almost an admission of failure when you have to have that sort of draconian regulation because your offering is so unattractive to the consumer that you must give them no choice; we also feel it is very bad marketing because we think wide screen should be offered as an exciting possibility for the European viewer not a threat to his pocket. You really confuse the message if you start to get a little bit too draconian.

Colin Shaw: Just before I ask Bryce to come in can I ask this? If we allow that the influence of politicians can either enhance or diminish the strength of a particular industry, if you were drawing up a league table of the weight of the industry in different countries and if as a layman I would see Japan at the top, what's the rest of the ranking?

Stephen Temple: I would say that in European terms the European industries are not too badly placed. I think in our particular industries Philips and Thomson are the leading players, although there are one or two players in Germany such as Bosch, and one or two others. I think there is a fear that unless we create the right conditions in Europe, the I made might not be the sort of statement I could make in seven or 10 years' time, and underpinning the worry of some civil servants in Brussels is the fact that underneath the consumer electronics industry you have the microelectronics industry and if you don't create the right conditions we could have a sort of domino effect where down goes the consumer electronics industry and as a consequence of that down goes the microelectronics industry which some see as vital to many other areas of the economy. So that's the sort of thing which is at stake in the arguments that are going on around this question of HDTV and MAC.

Colin Shaw: And is there a British industry somewhere in Europe?

Stephen Temple: I would say that in terms of a British-owned industry in consumer electronics the answer is no; we had Ferguson and they were taken over by Thomson. We've obviously got the bits of Philips which exist within the U.K., and it's our viewpoint that it is economic activity that matters rather than share ownership which is now coming more and more widely dispersed. If you mean British in the sense of research and development and manufacturing the answer is yes, and one has to say in that context that we also have Japanese companies in the U.K. making a very valuable contribution to our economy.

Bryce McCrirrick: It is nearly four years since I retired and therefore I am not talking on behalf of the BBC but am talking on behalf of myself and myself only.

I would like to put a slightly different emphasis on the high definition situation from my two colleagues but really I'm really taking up the points that they have actually made and changing their emphasis.

John talked about screens in one's home; we have sets today, and with a large set, say a 27 inch diagonal on 625, if it's a good set you'll get a very good definition and for normal viewing high definition does not add all that much. High definition however will be necessary when we have larger screens. When will we have larger screens? You can't get a cathode ray tube very easily into the home which is much bigger than about 27" diagonal. A 33" television set will not actually go through a door satisfactorily in the normal house. It weighs something like 500 lbs. So really we are looking for a new type of screen altogether, something which will be say 4 ft horizontally, whatever the height is to give us an aspect ratio of about 16:9 and about two inches thick so you can hang it up on the wall like a picture. It might be in the centre of the room rather as the fireplace was at one time.

Now we are 10 years away from that actually being an item which can be bought at a reasonable price. Not only that, although the broadcasters all say they want to go ahead with high definition, there is not one broadcaster in Europe who seriously wants to go ahead with high definition. There is not one in the world who is seriously thinking about going ahead at this moment, apart from NHK in Japan.

Therefore we shouldn't be thinking about the high definition system that we want to have in Europe within the next few years; we should be looking towards the end of the decade and what opportunities that gives us. Going back in history a little, in 1970 Japan started a long term project on high definition television. It was a 20-year programme and it cost something like $800 million. NHK is the main broadcaster and public service broadcaster in Japan, rather like the BBC is in this country. NHK is currently running a high definition system; it is the 1125 lines 60 fields system, and they're actually running it on a daily basis, a few hours each day. It is not catching on very well; they've had enough difficulties – one of the satellites has gone down and though they really wanted to have three channels, they've only got one. The sets cost about £15,000 and there are only about 100 of them in the market place in Japan, to look at this service.

In 1986 Japan put forward to the CCIR (the standards organization where every country is represented, we're represented by the DTI and it meets about every four years) the concept of 1125/60. It was fully supported by America because they're on 60 cycle mains supply exactly like Japan, but Europe argued against it and therefore it did not go through with the CCIR as a single high definition standard for the world.

Now Europe in arguing against it to a large extent used the excuse that any pictures from 1125/60 system would have to go through a standards converter to 50 fields for a British system, if the same programmes had to be used in our 625 service and changing fields is difficult. We argued on that basis, but quite truthfully we were really worried about the future of the electronic industry in Europe and that was our real concern. Immediately after this we started a programme called Eureka 95 in Europe to work on producing a new standard for Europe. In the meantime the IBA had done a lot of work on a new system called MAC. The government set up a small committee which decided that the United Kingdom DBS would actually be on MAC rather than on PAL. There are various reasons why the MAC picture is rather better than PAL, there is no doubt about that, and when BSB came on the air in the direct broadcasting satellite band it had to use MAC. However, before BSB came on the air, there were two other satellites, Kopernikus, a German satellite, and Astra, and they actually emerged as the dominant satellites as far as delivering programmes into the home was concerned. BSB collapsed, and both Kopernikus and Astra are transmitting in PAL, which has become the *de facto* standard.

Eureka 95 wanted a compatible system of high definition; in other words, a programme put out on 1125 lines could be received by people with their 625-line sets, whereas if you had a high definition set you'd get it in your own sparkling high definition. Therefore the work of Eureka was based on a compatible extension of MAC. If however there is no MAC the work of Eureka will not be compatible. Unless the EC Commissioners agree at the end of this year that all transmissions have got to be in MAC, I think the MAC window is now closed.

Going back however to a situation where we're not really looking in Europe for a high definition system until about the end of the decade, we should be thinking about what will be possible at that time.

In America, they started saying to themselves, we've been left behind here, we're going to have all the sets in America coming in from Japan; perhaps we should be thinking about it again. There is a combination of the computer companies and the Telecom people in America working together and there are about six different proposals at the moment being worked on in America. Two of them are completely digital; an important one is being developed by AT&T and Zenith and another one

4 Whose hands on the button?

by GE. Our hope is that it will work, as GE in America are confident it will; the bandwidth compression will be such that on one satellite transponder you would be able to put out a full high definition service or about six normal 625-line services. With this kind of compression you're not only talking about feeding satellites; it could be used on cable systems, it could be used on terrestrial services because it repackages the television picture in a much smaller bandwidth and therefore making it easy to get it through cables and terrestrial systems through which high definition will not easily go at the moment.

So the way forward should be that we should be looking very carefully at the work that is going on in America. There is another Eureka project, 256, which is looking at digital high definition. We should try to work with the Americans and try to achieve a single digital standard which might be available in about 10 years' time as a practical thing. In the meantime we should be doing work – as it is happening in Germany and in the United Kingdom – to improve the the terrestrial PAL signal that we've got at the moment. There are a lot of things that one can do to the PAL signal. The only problem we have is that there is a great difference of view about how we actually treat the aspect ratio. Do we have letterbox transmissions? Some parts of Europe are quite happy to have that because they are quite used to seeing films in that way. The public in this country doesn't like letterbox, therefore I think most probably we'll produce an extended PAL with PAL Plus, as opposed to Germany which will be partially a letterbox format but not completely.

Colin Shaw: It seems to me that what you're prescribing is a rather leisurely progress and I just wonder whether either John or Stephen feels that that leisurely progress is politically and economically tenable.

Stephen Temple: I would say both economically and technically it is not good to stop the clock for 10 years, but there are things that could be going on and I think the Germans are very keen on this question of changing the aspect ratio as the first step to HDTV; they think that there is a sufficient market interest for people to want to watch films. Our broadcasters particularly cut bits off the film to match the TV frame, so you're not actually seeing the full picture that you would see in the cinema.

There is also a view that sport would benefit. Our sympathies are that if the broadcasters and set manufacturers want to have a crack at that market and MAC is really the thing that will do that quickly, let them have a go, and that can fill the market space in the next 10 years, and then by the end of the decade either MAC has got such a foothold that John's evolutionary route can then build it up to a high definition form of MAC or digital will come round the corner and zap it and it will come that way.

Bryce McCrirrick: I'm not saying stop for 10 years; I'm even going further than you and suggesting that we put all our efforts in the short term into an expanded PAL, which we can actually use it on our existing services at the moment. That's the important thing. We start work, or we continue work on the digital system now, but accept the fact that we will most probably not have anything real for another 10 years.

John Forrest: On the economic aspects over the next 10 years, I think whatever the broadcasters do we shall see high definition television introduced in the recorded

53

medium either on tape or on disc, very much associated with this liaison of the film makers and the industry, particularly the Japanese industry.

George Cook: I find myself in the embarrassing situation of agreeing with everything that the DTI have said, and there is a first for industry and DTI.

Just picking up Bryce's point for a moment, I can remember when I worked for him, we used to go to Japan and we came back and we said when is the large screen high definition display going to appear, and as he said five years. And we were saying that five years ago. I think perhaps 10 years is too long now; I think it may be about five years away. Eureka is a consortium of Western European manufacturers who are producing equipment for a 1250/50 high definition service. I find it very interesting that we go to meetings with our friends from Germany, France and the rest of Europe and we reach an accord with the dastardly French. This is something that came as a tremendous surprise to us all, that we could agree standards so quickly. One of the things that Europe can be very proud of is the way in which this consortium has got together in a very short time to develop a full range of high definition equipment which rivals that of the Japanese.

I personally believe that an evolutionary approach in marketing terms could be wrong for one very simple reasons: I think that if one can see Wimbledon on the present 625-line receiver, there is little incentive to go out and pay a very large amount of money for a new receiver. In order to get people to do that you have to consider an elitist service, and I think the way that high definition television will best be marketed is that it will be a service that is only available on high definition and not available on any other channel.

Colin Shaw: I would like briefly to to talk about the possibility of the BBC's transmission function after 1996 being taken away in the way that transmission functions has been taken away from the ITC/IBA.

John Forrest: Since time is short perhaps I can just identify what I think was a slightly special situation in the independent sector in that regulation and transmission were combined, very much part of the same organization under the IBA, whereas programme making was separate from that organization in the terrestrial franchise holders. Keeping together regulation and transmission was fine as long as one was dealing with one technology or one particular family of broadcasters.

When DBS came along and the IBA was responsible for what were in essence competing programme streams by satellite and by terrestrial and the engineering and transmission function was then starting to have to address rather different customers with rather different requirements, it became very difficult to consider keeping a structure with regulation and transmission so tightly entwined. There was also the aspect that one was seeing in the general world an increasing overlap of telecommunications and broadcasting and again to have that transmission function exclusively tied to this one family of broadcasters would seem to imply it becoming less and less efficient, less and less able to exploit its staff and its assets in wider markets to the benefit of those new markets and to the benefit of its existing customers.

So I think in that sense it's a very positive step to be able to take this transmission function away from the regulatory function, remove the conflicts between those two and allow the transmission function now to have what is in essence the right relationship, a commercial relationship with the broadcasters in handling their signal for the last stage of transmission to the viewer and liberating an organization to allow it to play a very exciting role in this new overlap area. Apart from the fact that there are certain losses – perhaps the change in character of the R&D is a danger here, and also one has now fragmented the structure a little bit – it does bring considerable benefits to the system as a whole.

Bryce McCrirrick: The government wanted to privatize the BBC's transmission depart-ment and it was actually mentioned in the government's green paper; the idea was to do it also in January of 1991. But when they looked at it a bit more carefully they found that it couldn't be done without the agreement of the BBC governors because of the charter and decided therefore to postpone any decision on this until 1996.

I think it probably will happen. I don't actually feel very strongly about this, but I would prefer that the BBC was allowed to make the decision itself. The government is screwing the BBC for money, its income over the next years is going to be increased by the RPI minus 3%. I think the BBC should be allowed to decide whether the transmission side should be done in house or contracted out and the BBC's decision should be based on the best value for money it can achieve.

John Forrest: If we were to move to a situation of trying to have two competing transmission companies in this country we have to take note of what is going on in other countries. If you take France for example, they are going in exactly the opposite direction. They are addressing the overlap of broadcasting and telecommunications by bringing together into a very dynamic force their broadcasting and telecommuni-cation transmission systems. We have to be a little bit careful about this great desire for competition leading to an excessive fragmentation which then essentially makes us very weak in European and world markets.

.   .   .

In discussion during this session, it was argued that the numbers game was very confusing to lay people. A speaker from Granada referred to that company's Wad-dington experiment, in which inhabitants of a whole village were supplied with high definition, satellite, cable and other choices. Participants were urged to read Gra-nada's report on the Waddington study, in which it was, briefly, concluded that if a programme is good, people will watch it. A wide-screen picture was, however, seen as an advantage, and current research suggested that the British did not mind a "letter-box" picture; perhaps the Germans were in this case right to argue that the audience wanted to see the whole film.

A speaker from another ITV company referred to BARB research which gave little or no evidence that people would be willing to pay extra for HDTV service.

It was pointed out that rooftop aerials were getting increasingly sophisticated and complicated.

From the platform, Stephen Temple responded that the importance of programme quality was recognized, but noted that there were gradations of demand, like a shelf containing increasingly expensive bottles of wine in a supermarket. He also noted that products like Vodafone illustrated that some people will buy advanced technology at literally any price.

Another issue, raised from the floor but not answered during the session, was that of liability for broadcast libels; was the private transmission agency responsible for such matters?

The session was warned that standardization was a complicated business that merged political and industrial interests. "Don't come crying to us that Brussels is about to rape you," said Stephen Temple.

Among those who participated in the discussion in this session were:

Richard Ellis, Granada TV
Chris Horsley, Yorkshire TV
David Rumble, PA Consulting Group
David Rushton, Institute of Local Television
Michael Starks, BBC
Gary Tonge, ITC
Murray Weston, British Universities Film & Video Council

5 The end of BBC radio as we know it?

Michael Green
Controller, BBC Radio 4

James Gordon
Radio Clyde

Gillian Reynolds
Daily Telegraph

Chair: John Gray
Independent consultant

John Gray: I'm ex-BBC but now I belong to that horrible breed of thing called a consultant (unfortunately, not enough people consult me, but we'll leave that particular plug aside).

Part of the ethos of the BBC which differentiates it very distinctly from commercial television is that it started as a radio service, and it had the ethos of a radio service built into it before it took on television, before it had a competitor. All the old clichés of radio have their truth: that the pictures are much better on radio, and that the level of conversation you get in the canteen of Radio 1 is of a higher intellectual level than you get in the canteen of a television organization. There is an element of truth in both these.

In the next four or five years what was the premier radio broadcasting organization of the world, to a greater extent perhaps than being the premier television broadcasting organization, is going to face a change of the nature of the organization, a change and a re-definition of its purposes and policies.

Radio, in a curious way, appeals to the two ends of the age scale of the audience. One bit of radio, largely catered for by the more commercial side and Radio 1, appeals to, and is to a greater extent run by, very young people. The other primary audience of radio tends to be the older and the alone who make very considerable demands on the informational and the intellectual standards of what they are getting. We still have probably the finest output; the greatest output of drama in this country is radio drama and it is not centred entirely on London. And it serves an immense audience compared to the audience in the theatre. So there are two extreme ends.

The other difference in radio is that ever since the initiation of the Regional Scheme of the BBC, the BBC has sought to serve the whole country. No other country really has achieved network coverage.

In the future we are going to face the financial problem – how is it going to paid for? – and there is the anomaly that the licence doesn't really cover radio. What is going to be the extent of the plethora of extension of radio? The Radio Authority is talking about another three hundred to four hundred stations within this decade. How are they going to be run? Are they going to be centralized? Even if the stations are independent and separate, the commercial sector is certainly growing larger.

It is interesting that in 1962 both John Gorst of the Local Radio Association, the commercial side, and the BBC experiments in local radio, both agreed for different reasons that the ideal audience for a small local station which would have a definable audience, was somewhere between seventy-five thousand and a quarter of a million. That has gone out of the window almost entirely except that the fringe possibilities of community radio are coming in.

These are the problems which will be facing us – money, the form of organization, what your target audiences are and how you serve them.

Michael Green: I'm not sure I can live up to John's prescription but I'll have a go. I come to you this morning as a broadcaster turned bureaucrat but, at least not knowingly, not one who consorts with dancing bishops as you might have surmised from the previous session.

If you want to feel the pulse of middle England, come on a journey through my in-tray. A couple of recent letters offer some useful insights into the special relationship between the listener and one BBC radio service. The first is about weather forecasts: "I know it is de rigueur for BBC executives to be post-Benthamite utilitarians trying to bring the greatest happiness to the greatest number. But I think people like you are wasting their time trying to jazz up weather bulletins." That letter, as you will have guessed, came from Hampstead.

The second concerns a piece of music familiar to the insomniacs among you called "Sailing By" which acts as a sort of homing beacon for stray mariners waiting for the late night shipping forecast. This correspondent points out that in the third bar of "Sailing By" the double bass player makes a mistake, then fails to appear at all in the fourth bar and only recovers in the fifth. "For years," he says, "this has been very amusing but no longer. Would it not now be possible for BBC engineers to find the appropriate note elsewhere in the piece, to copy it and to insert it in the third bar? Or is it the case that insertion of the right note will be the signal to the Royal Navy that the balloon has gone up?"

Well, as that completely unscientific sample reveals, radio in this country still matters. Video has not killed the radio star, as the pop song would have it. Across the Atlantic the lack of consistent public funding on any scale, the absence of networks as we know them and the fragmentation of services to fill a thousand niches have all contributed to the diminished role and influence of American radio.

In this country, almost three-quarters of the population, about forty million people, tuned in at some point each week during the last quarter of 1990. And all recent opinion research points to a deep and abiding public affection for radio. We may no longer attract the fourteen million listeners who used to tune in regularly on Sundays to *The Clitheroe Kid* – actually not many television shows can produce that sort of audience these days – but we've survived the video age as much more than a minority sport.

But I recognize that survival is sometimes hard won. We talk about a period of change. Radio has been in a generation of change. The BBC monopoly as some of you knew it came to an end thirty years ago with the onslaught of commercial television. We lost the monopoly in ideas and talent and the raids on radio's intellectual and creative reserves have gone on ever since. Our capacity for fattening chickens for the television market, particularly if they can tell jokes, is well noted. Since then the BBC's role as the dominant strategic player has been challenged first by the pirates, then by BBC local stations and ILR which have offered formidable competition to network services. And the pace of adapting to a changing market place has accelerated to the point, now, where we enter the toughest competitive decade head to head with up to three national commercially funded radio networks. Our network monopoly is about to disappear. I welcome that. Frankly, it's long overdue. The creation of a national market place offers the best prospect of putting this medium on the editorial and political agenda, of raising its profile in the public consciousness.

It should also help to secure radio's share of funding, whether from advertising or from the licence fee, at a time when television's need of nourishment is going to increase dramatically. And it's self-evident, too, that any broadcaster with a clean sheet of paper has the opportunity in theory, at least, to show that the boundaries of what's possible in radio can, and should, be extended.

For us the whiff of competition is in our nostrils. As a result of the green paper in 1988, we have been forced to reflect on the nature of the services we offer and how we arrange them. The market has pushed us towards greater clarity of purpose already. The loss of frequencies, as you know, means that we are becoming primarily an FM service with an unprecedented programme of capital development for transmitters to support it. We created Radio 5 in part to stop the confusing pattern of frequency splitting which bedevilled Radio 2 and Radio 4 in the past. We are at the same time exhorted to end simulcasting whenever possible and, indeed, only Radio 4 will, in future, enjoy the luxury of two frequencies beyond next year. And the value of preserving two frequencies, I think, was fairly vividly demonstrated during the Gulf War when we were able to launch Radio 4 News FM, and we shall be discussing further how we exploit this luxury in listener choice.

Now, despite the shift towards a better ordering of our broadcasting affairs, it's inevitable that the BBC will lose market share. It happened to BBC Television, it's already happening to us. We have now around 65%. We expect that to fall to 50% by the mid-1990s. And this decline will of course be taking place in a climate of debate about the future of the licence fee itself. What claim can BBC radio make to continued public funding? What are the arguments for the current level of public service broadcasting in an expanded radio market?

I want to emphasize at this point that the philosophy of what we have we hold is no longer justifiable, if it ever was. Public service never was a synonym for the BBC. ILR stations too seek to occupy the high editorial ground. Each BBC service has to justify itself in terms of the distinctiveness of its voice and of audience satisfaction with its programmes. And at the same time, the strength of the case lies in the totality of the service, the fact that it is seen at some time to offer something to most listeners. It's the diversity of the schedule across five networks and local radio which means at the moment that four out of five listeners tune in, at some point, to a BBC service each week. If patronage of our channels were to be able to remain at that level, despite a diminishing market share, if our programmes retain a continuing high degree of acceptability, I think we have a case to put to the public.

The argument for the preservation of Radios 3 and 4 gets the easier ride, I find. Large scale support for writers, musicians, performers and programme makers of all kinds is seen as a cultural act in the widest sense and forces radio onto the stage. It allows radio to be taken seriously. Indeed, actually I would argue that without investment in diverse and attractive speech programmes in particular, radio is not a credible medium. It would become here, as in so many other places, simply another juke box in the corner. What linger in the folk memory, in the wireless folk memory, are *The Goons*, *The Hitchhiker's Guide*, *After Henry*, *Adrian Mole* – programmes developed and sustained by risk-taking investment. And I use the word risk-taking not to suggest for one moment that I inhabit the same difficult world of the balance sheet as Jimmy Gordon, far from it, but to convey the idea that the joy of the licence fee is to allow the broadcaster to allocate resources as he sees fit, without any knowledge *a priori* of whether or not there's a public appetite for what he is going to do. It gives me the ability, for example, to make five hundred plays and launch fifty new dramatists a year, and for John Drummond on Radio 3 to commission new work for the Proms. That's a privilege to be exercised with care and with conviction.

There is, I believe, a widely held view that what's at stake here is some kind of public good deserving patronage. If BBC Radio in the United Kingdom is to continue to be a market maker, not necessarily the market maker, but a market maker, there has to be investment in programmes of quality which, in turn, means a long term commitment to people and to technology. Now whenever the subject of funding this kind of radio arises, the eyes of even the most hardened market economists grow moist. Professor Peacock sought refuge in his Public Service Broadcasting Council as a way of securing the future of Radio 3 and 4. *The Economist* recently argued for the replacement of the licence fee by subscription but confessed that this solution still left what is rather quaintly called "the tricky problem of radio." Government legislation has acknowledged that an alternative to the public purse for radio has not yet been found. Now there are those who argue that the size of the public purse could be reduced if BBC Radio limited itself to providing services which the market couldn't deliver. Peacock's recommendation, you will remember, that Radios 1 and 2 be privatized and financed by advertisements has been echoed in recent papers from the political right and it will go on. And for some it's an attractive proposition since it leaves the field open for the heavy guns of commerce. For other it will consign the BBC to producing everything that is commercially unviable and, at a stroke, eliminate the BBC's largest audiences.

Our strength is our ability to serve all constituents on a significant scale. Radios 1 and

2, it can be argued, are as much the centre of gravity in their own areas as Radios 3 and 4 even though the tide of competition is lapping round their ankles. Radio 1's commitment to news and current affairs, to social action programmes, to documentaries charting the history of pop music and so on – all that offers something special in a crowded market place. On Radio 2 Jimmy Young is as important to the coverage of public affairs as any of the Radio 4 sequences. If INR 1 turns out to resemble Radio 2 most closely, what will be its attitude to specialist music programmes, to the arts and to the regions?

There are two further considerations I would like to put to you. The first is that the breadth of output that we offer is such that all age groups are reached in, more or less, equal measure. The impact of Radio 2 and BBC local radio on the older listener is very significant. The pattern for commercial radio, as I observe it, is markedly different, with weekly reach peaking at about 50-odd per cent for the 16-24 year olds and declining to about 16% amongst the over 65s. And in the commercial world the elderly, and their need for radio, must surely be vulnerable.

Whatever aspirations ILR and INR may have to serve the whole audience, the preference of advertisers must surely be to target those with high disposable incomes. They are unlikely to touch, in any significant way, either the over 65s or the under 16s, both groups, incidentally, massively under-represented in the total listening profile; someone should, in my view.

The second consideration is this: the received wisdom about listening habits is that once people discover a station which most meets their needs, they stay loyal to it. This wisdom has defined programme policy for many years and, in some respects, it's squeezed commissioning editors into much narrower editorial bands than was good for the health of the networks. Recent research, however, presents a quite different picture of loyalty and attachment. In fact a high degree of promiscuity is going on among radio listeners. 20% of the Radio 4 audience now listens to Radio 1 each week. 26% of them listen to ILR and conversely about 70% of the ILR audience tunes into a BBC service at some point during the average week. There is, in fact, a greater degree of over-lap now between Radio 4 and Radio 1 listeners than between Radio 4 and Radio 3. Today's audiences are refusing to be type-cast, tastes cannot any longer be neatly parcelled up. I believe that we should no longer imagine that by providing radio services of one brow level through the licence fee and letting so-called popular radio go to market we would necessarily satisfy listeners' expectations of the public purse.

There's no evidence yet that the public wants BBC radio to do less. Andrew Ehrenberg and Pam Mills in their study of viewers' willingness to pay, because it is the television licence that we are talking about, found no support from the market for the idea of cutting services in order to reduce the licence fee. In radio the public attitude seems to be that we should do more whether by serving ethnic communities, children or providing a continuous service of news during the Gulf War. And despite the well-rehearsed misgivings about the BBC's role in local radio, I see no evidence either that the public wants the BBC to retreat there. As someone who began his BBC career in local radio, I've sometimes felt that the service did itself less than justice by appearing to be more a substitute for the DSS than a broadcasting institution. But the recent shift of emphasis towards journalism as the priority serving a community's appetite for information about its own backyard gives at long last the BBC's role a sharper focus. The provision of news, so expensive to put in place and to sustain, so crucial at local level, seems sadly to be the first casualty of recession in the commercial sector of radio. Good journalism, rather than the cheaper currency of music, will distinguish the BBC voice in the burgeoning world of local and community radio.

We march on a very broad front. Whether we continue to do so depends on whether listeners go on voting for us with their tuning fingers. And the question facing public and politicians is this: given the added value of radio broadcasting in this country, are five network services worth a pound a month? Is the preservation of public radio, a fading flower in so many places, worth that amount? If it isn't, at what level do you want it? We need to think hard about the funding of radio in its own right, not as a postscript to the television debate. Are there market mechanisms now widespread in the public sector generally which might be appropriate to radio and not to television? What, for this medium, is the price of continuing purity?

As the public makes up its mind, and in the end the public will have to make its mind up, we are paddling furiously below the surface. Radio, as we have known it, has been an extraordinary slumbering beast. The conservatism of production forces mirrored precisely the conservatism of audience taste. The result was inertia. One woman, commenting on my decision to move Woman's Hour to the morning, observed that it would "not be possible to listen to a discussion about female orgasm at 10.30 in the morning." 2 o'clock was fine.

Things are moving, though it may not yet be the earth. We are becoming more competitive, sometimes to the irritation of those who prefer a more sober opponent. We need to win converts to editorial change and innovation, while recognising that it is the sense of continuity and permanence that actually draws people to this particular medium. As money gets tighter, even within the present framework, we shall have to find ways of making some of our programmes more cheaply and more efficiently. There will, I hope, always be Rolls Royces in the garage but not everything has to be gold-plated. There is still the huge challenge of winning the seven million people in whose lives radio plays no part whatsoever at the moment.

We need to open our doors to producers outside the BBC. If the free market can't function properly because of spectrum shortage in radio, at least not for some time, we have to find a way, as television is finding, of allowing more people in. Independent production will be a growing feature of BBC radio in the mid 1990s.

Competition is troubling but energising. And if the spirit of the green paper and subsequent legislation is observed, I think we shall be propelled into a world of improving quality and extended choice not one of imitation and editorial retreat. I believe that in this mixed economy, a strong BBC Radio, much as we know it today, is worth fighting for. I believe it will be needed and valued by all sides in the new environment.

James Gordon: First of all can I say that I agree with literally almost everything Michael Green said? Indeed, as a great admirer of the BBC and one who, as a listener and viewer, would be quite content for it to remain as it is, I'm glad that the somewhat provocative title of this session is followed by a question mark. Because if we interpret "we" as the listening and viewing public, I do not think that the changes that will occur in BBC Radio or BBC Television will be nearly as cataclysmic as some people fear. If, however, we interpret "we" in the title to mean BBC insiders, or what has been referred to here as broadcasting's chattering classes, then fundamental change is inevitable.

It is sensible to look first of all at the size and composition of the total listening audience. This is a reflection of our different research systems, but we think the total audience for radio is slightly higher than the BBC think it is, although we don't have much argument about who's got what share. Let me take my own experience in Central Scotland, which is the worst possible territory for radio because it has got the highest hours viewed to BBC 1, BBC 2, ITV and Channel 4. In our area we suffered, as did the BBC, from the introduction of breakfast television; audiences fell. But the introduction of 24-hour television has not seriously impacted on our audiences after 9 o'clock. It is reasonable to assume that the introduction of further TV services will affect radio only slightly but will further fragment television audience. It would be foolish, however, to anticipate any real growth in the listening audience. It follows that the introduction of further services will simply cut the existing cake into thinner slices. For the independent sector, dependent as it is on advertising revenue, it's clearly vital to us that that growth comes at the expense of listening to the BBC rather than simply cannibalising the existing audience to commercial radio.

Now the well-publicized changes in the demographics of the population are already being reflected in programming in both sections. Radios 1 and 2 in the BBC have both arguably moved up the age scale slightly and in the independent sector, where most stations have been pleasantly surprised by the success of appealing to an older age group with their gold services. And if we look at the so-called incremental stations, it is significant that by far the most successful has been Melody Radio in London appealing to an older age group. Even in commercial terms, Michael's fears about the older end of the population being ignored can be allayed.

The fact is that the baby boomers have become the thirtysomethings and just as the BBC was caught out in the early 1960s by the rise in teenage numbers and discretionary spending power, so in my view among the most successful stations in the 1990s will be those who cater for the mature market. The tyranny of the teenage record buyer in station playlists may well be on the way out.

Now we can say with some certainty that there are going to be more radio stations in 10 years' time than there are now, though, in my view, not nearly as many as some people are predicting. How we are to ensure that the new services extend listener choice, rather than simply duplicate what is already available, will in the long run be decided by listeners themselves. But it would be a great help if the regulatory system encouraged choice. I have believed for some time that a Radio Authority encompassing all radio would be more likely to optimize use of scarce frequencies, to extend the range of services available to listeners, and, as far as possible, acknowledge the availability of additional funding in the pace at which it introduced new services. Without an overall authority, new services might simply replicate those already provided by the BBC. Alternatively, of course, there's nothing to stop the BBC altering its output to pre-empt the schedule about to be presented or provided by a new INR service or a new local service. BBC Radio and the independent radio sector combined would still be dwarfed by both BBC television and ITV. Both of us have got to fight for our resources against our respective big brothers in broadcasting. There is much that we could do together.

It is worthwhile recalling that five members of the Annan committee, which reported in March 1977, advocated the separation of BBC Radio from BBC Television in the interests of efficient management of the BBC itself. This argument for the moment has been lost and perhaps the greater synergy there is in news gathering between radio and television might keep it that way. But the BBC, I think, will be encouraged to know that broadcasting ministers probably grossly over-estimate the lobbying power of the BBC among Conservative backbenchers and certainly peers; they are scared stiff to touch it, or certainly were last time around. However, as the BBC digests the experience of having surrendered some frequencies which are now going to be used for national radio and finding that it actually derives income by so doing, the arguments may well be re-examined in the run-up to 1996. Given the prospect of actually earning revenue, rather than spending money, by surrendering some fre-quencies and sites, I imagine that every BBC service, both local and national, will have to re-justify its existence.

The BBC perhaps survived longer than it should have done with only two national services. But it is quite important, if you are looking at the public service principle, to recognize that the introduction of the Third Programme of itself paved the way for the move to the American vertical model of Radios 1, 2, 3 and 4 and away from the Reithian idea of mixed programming on single frequencies. The creation of local radio also recognized that in a television age programming would, to a large extent, replace programmes and that the utilitarian role of radio in providing information can best be done at a local level. The move to life-style radio, if you like, during radio's peak time recognizes the primacy of television essentially in the provision of programmes in the traditional sense.

There might, therefore, be a useful parlour game for future Symposia: assume that the BBC were compelled either by the Home Office or by its own internal KGB Finance Committee to surrender one national radio frequency – which should go?

Now – not just because Michael is here – may I say that the case for retaining Radio 4 is, in my view, overwhelming? National resources, and very substantial ones at that, are required for the gathering and dissemination of news. Of the three music channels I concede, obviously, that Radios 1 and 2 could either be run by the independent sector or could take advertising which might amount to the same thing, or alternatively that the service could be provided at a local level with the added benefit of local informa-tion. But although we in the independent sector are justifiably proud of our share of the listening audience, I've always regarded it as very significant that quite so many people want to continue to listen to Radio 1 and Radio 2 despite the fact that they tell the people in my area absolutely nothing that is relevant to Glasgow. That is an immense tribute to the professionalism of Radio 1 and Radio 2. So the BBC are entitled to say that in order to maintain a public service they should retain Radio 1 and Radio 2. It's much less easy to justify the retention of Radio 3, certainly in its present form with a share of total listening of under 2 per cent. I think there might be a strong case for amalgamating Radio 3 and Radio 4 to provide a single first-class service eliminating perhaps the softer elements of Radio 4's output, and the more patronising, if not downright intimidating, aspects of Radio 3's.

Some people, however, think that the axe is going to fall on BBC local radio. It is more important to look at the service itself rather than at who provides it or how it's funded. BBC local radio tends to serve areas which are large by comparison with those of ILR. I think they could be privatized and would be viable, with advertising as a source of funding, particularly if this were phased in over, say, three years.

You see the real case for the duality of funding, as mentioned in an intervention this morning, the licence fee for the BBC and advertising for the independent sector, is the scarcity of advertising revenue. But from my point of view, and this is naked self-interest, if by public policy we are going to be required to have more services in any event, I would much rather have advertising on the BBC than have the BBC remain as a no-go area for advertisers thus reducing the overall profile of radio and making it less likely that our share of the advertising cake would grow. This point is quite crucial when people bemoan radio as the 2% medium in this country compared with over 6% in the United States. The fact is that independent radio in this country takes just over a third share of total listening to radio; the rest is BBC. Simple mathematics indicate that if advertising were available on all radio in this country, that 2% would rise to 6% – almost exactly what it is in the United States.

Whatever happens, it is almost certain that BBC's share of total listening will decline somewhat; it is at the moment hovering around 60% and probably will decline to 50% or just under. But I have much too high a regard for the BBC to assume that it is going to fall to, say, under 25%. From a self-interested point of view of radio as an advertising medium, and given that although people do switch they're still less promiscuous than television viewers, it's going to be that bit more difficult for radio to make the quantum leap in its appeal to advertisers if a significant proportion of the total radio audience cannot be reached by advertisers. In short, with more independent services, we face both further fragmentation of the audience and competition for advertising revenue but still the BBC as a no-go area.

With advertising on the BBC, OK, we face extra competition for advertising revenue, which we are going to have anyway, but the audiences are less fragmented and we have the advantage of reaching the entire radio listening population. I don't believe that the source of funding is of itself vital to the public service ethos. The drive for higher ratings is motivated, in my view, almost entirely by professional self-respect. If BBC local radio has sizeable audiences, and in many areas it has, it could be a viable commercial service and the integrity of its output could be protected by enforcing strict adherence to a Promise of Performance which reflected its current output.

Since most of BBC local radio opts in and out of national services this would be a further argument either for an overall Radio Authority or for, at least, a fairly close working commercial relationship between BBC radio and the independent sector.

Now I have concentrated on the BBC because that was the dominant theme of the Symposium but I think, in the light of John's introductory remarks, it's appropriate that, in conclusion, I should say something about the future of the independent sector, which is far from clear. Recent attempts by the Radio Authority to define pop music have simply shown that Earl Ferrers, in the House of Lords, was much nearer the mark with his definition of "thump, thump, thump". I think, however, that the Radio Authority was right to make the only FM INR service one which was non-pop. If properly run it should take its audience from Radio 2, not existing ILR audiences, and thus improve the overall profile of radio as an advertising medium to advertisers. Nor do I think that a national pop music station would necessarily be more successful. I don't think a pop INR station would achieve the same audience levels as Radio 1 or, for that matter, local ILR stations which offer a pop service on one frequency. It is at last dawning on applicants for franchises that they are not starting with a blank sheet of paper. Radio listening is probably finite in quantity and they will only gain an audience at the expense of some of the existing services.

Total radio listening in this country is just as high as in any other country. Those who argue for many more services on the pattern of the United States ignore one fundamental fact. A station in the United States will pay approximately 3% of its revenue in copyright charges to the equivalent of the Performing Rights Society representing composers. It will pay nothing at all to the record companies. A station the size of Radio Clyde pays about 6% to the composers and slightly more than that to the record companies – a total of 12%. Now that differential of 9% of revenue over stations in the United States vitally affects the number of stations you can afford.

At the moment a third of the stations in America do not make money. Recently at the U.S. Budget Summit there was talk of a spectrum tax of 4% of revenue. The radio industry was up in arms and successfully lobbied and resisted the proposal on the grounds that if there was a 4% spectrum tax, the number of loss-making stations would go up to over 50%. Now that's with 4% extra, not the 9% differential I'm referring to here; what would that do to radio in the United States? In my view the number of stations would go down to a third, or less, of the current number.

Forget about 300 stations in Britain. It is not going to happen. There is simply not the advertising revenue to fund them. Nor is it desirable to have radio formats so narrow that the listener's horizons are never broadened.

I attended a recent meeting in the United States of the National Association of Broadcasters. There were separate programme seminars on all formats. There was one on Adult Contemporary, there was another one on Soft Adult Contemporary and, yet a third, on New Adult Contemporary. Now I recognize the importance of packaging in marketing but it seems to me, in this case, we are talking of a distinction without a difference.

We are at an important stage in the development of local radio. Until now our appeal has been mainly geographical – the greater relevance of our news and information compared with national networks. Now I think we are at the beginning of what could be a sea-change in which the generic appeal of the particular music format, which has hitherto been the main attraction of national services, might also be what happens with local. It follows, therefore, that there could be great synergy between stations that are far apart geographically but use the same music format. And, indeed, the narrower the format, the greater the geographical base you need for survival.

Jazz FM, for example, whose problems in London have been well publicized, might make it in London – might. It certainly won't make it outside any major metropolitan area in Britain. Therefore if you want jazz available to the entire population, it's either going to have to be a national frequency or there's going to be a string of stations with the central one probably based in London, simply because it is the largest area, feeding either actual programming or at least playlists to the rest of its network of jazz stations throughout most areas.

Now we are also surely at the point at which the Radio Authority must really give more serious consideration to the financial viability of applicants for local radio. Just over two years ago I caused some eyebrows to be raised, which I didn't mind, but also some offence to be caused, which I did mind, by predicting that 25% of the incremental stations would be broke within two years. That's proved to be a gross under-estimate. I must stress that I really am not hostile to the concept of community radio. Indeed I regard Radio Clyde as a community radio station. I do believe that in many cases the demand for such services comes, however, not from listeners but from those who want to provide the service. And I'm bolstered in that view by the Broadcast Research Unit's Report where on page 145 it says, having said already that more localized neighbourhood stations didn't excite many listeners, it went on to state that 18% of those who wanted new neighbourhood stations expressed an interest in running them and 33% in helping to make occasional programmes. Now that suggests to me rather a profligate use of scarce frequencies and a ratio between programme maker and listener that does not augur well for the financial future of these smaller neighbourhood stations. If, however, somebody wants to run them, good luck to them – but I don't think they are entitled to rely on a subsidy from the rest of the industry or on tax payers' funds.

In this connection it is interesting to note that I think last week the Radio Authority advertised Pitlochry and Aberfeldy, a lovely part of the world – total adult population 5,000. Assume that a station there achieves 100% reach. Everybody there listens to it, every week. Assume also that they've got 100% share – nobody listens any more to the BBC, all radio listening is entirely to them. Go further and assume that they derive twice the level of local advertising pounds per thousand listener hours of any station in Scotland. I still don't see how they can make ends meet.

This poses a policy dilemma. Does every area in Britain, irrespective of size, have the right to its own local radio service irrespective of viability? Bear in mind that most areas are capable of almost endless sub-division with probably an increasing sense of community identity as the areas get smaller. And I speak as one who believes that the universality of provision of national radio and television is, in fact, the corner-stone of the public service ethos. If you look at what has happened with mobile telephone networks you get a very good idea of what services would be provided on radio and television in my part of the world had it been left entirely to commercial forces. Whole areas of Scotland wouldn't have any. The BBC and the Independent Broadcasting Authority have spent huge sums of money bringing these national services to literally every corner of the UK. Some people would argue that the same logic should apply to local radio. Now I disagree and I think this issue needs to be exposed.

I think there is a clear distinction between national radio and local radio. I think that it is right that national radio, to merit that name, should be obliged to reach all corners of the nation and not simply concentrate on metropolitan areas where transmission costs per thousand of population are under one per cent of what they are in some parts of Scotland. On the other hand I don't believe it is realistic to say that every community has the right to define itself as a community, irrespective of size, and demand a local radio service as a right. Make no mistake, community is not a term capable of absolute and exact definition. I am a citizen of the UK; surprise – I am also a Scot. I'm a Glaswegian with a distinct preference, frankly, for the north of the river. And, while much too sensible to believe in the concept of a master race, I am, if pressed, willing to admit that I could be wrong and it might well reside in the North-Western corner of Glasgow.

Where do you stop? I believe that the expectations of some very decent public-spirited citizens have been artificially raised by the advertising of some contracts by the IBA and now the Radio Authority. However many caveats they put in saying there is no guarantee it will work, people believe that if it has been advertised there must be some way of making it work. And, frankly, the experience of the incremental system so far shows that that simply isn't true; there isn't a way of making it work. And the sooner the Radio Authority injects a note of realism into the proceedings, the better.

Gillian Reynolds: I'm grateful for the acknowledgement that radio has at last come into its own and is increasingly being acknowledged as a major cultural force and influence. But let's look at what's there; you turn on your radio now and there are an awful lot of people clearly fostering some unrealistic expectations. In London you can dial up and down, and you can find about a dozen stations on either AM or FM; this morning I listened to about a dozen altogether on AM and FM here in Manchester. You hear as you dial up and down a lot of music. You hear a lot of chat – I won't say it's speech broadcasting – you hear a lot of chat. I heard Alan Deswick on GMR, I heard Sunset Radio doing a promotion with Body Shop products; I heard last week listening to BBC Radio Merseyside Billy and Wally, "the number one turn in Local Radio"; I listened the other week to Norman Thomas on BBC Radio Lancashire. Norman Thomas got his first job in radio from me when I was programme controller at Radio City and I have to tell you, if he still worked for me, he would have been fired that afternoon. There is lots and lots and lots of music.

The other day I was talking to a man from the PRS, and I asked him, because his is the unenviable job of monitoring what is on radio in the way of music, as you go up and down the country, and everyone now has got a Gold Service, and an FM service, can you tell the difference between the Gold Services, and he said there's scarcely a pin to chose; it's Elvis and it's Cliff and the playlists are more or less the same. There is a bit more difference in the FM services. So though there is a lot of chat, a lot of music and there are some places that still offer programmes as opposed to programming and that is mostly the BBC, now I'm most intrigued to find that radio listeners are more promiscuous that we had hitherto believed and they do tune around.

I've been promiscuous in my habits for many a long year and derive great pleasure from it, but I do find that radio does have a particular effect on you, you get very fond of it. So when you speak about it, I tend, even though I listen in any given day to Radio 3, Radio 4, Radio 2, bit of Radio 1, bit of Capital, bit of this, bit of that, bit of Kiss but

I still tend to talk mostly about my favourite which is usually Radio 4. Roger Bolton, yesterday, talking about stuffy Radio 4 was clearly talking from the greatest of affection and it's an interesting fact to remark on. He also said that he would like to see more competition in the Radio 4 line, he would like to see more people doing speech programmes. Now those few of you who listened to City Talk, which was a brave attempt at Radio City in Liverpool to make it a mainly speech service, will have been as disappointed as I was. Good talk costs money, good talk is not thin air; it takes production, it takes thought, it takes imagination, it takes time, it takes studio time and commercial radio either can't or won't afford it. LBC in London diversified into two services on AM and FM and you listen to both of them, and they are no competition for Radio 4. They are chat radio; they are not structured speech radio. It was interesting while the Gulf War was on to make the totally invidious comparison between Radio 4 News FM which has total air supremacy and LBC. So I think Roger Bolton might wait a long time to see competition for Radio 4 coming from the independent sector.

We come here to the question of the definition of public service. Is it local information? Is it reliable news? Is it doing what the market can't or won't provide? Is it the sort of programmes that you wouldn't get anywhere else? Now elements of this do exist on some commercial radio stations. Jimmy has produced and still produces drama, still produces documentary. Moray Firth Radio consistently wins prizes, and Capital Radio has distinguished itself in recent years by going back to programme making. Is it something that delights the people who work there?

The problem then comes – where do you put it on the air? If you are programming using advertising as your funding you have to reach certain numbers and certain kinds of audiences. If that audience is paying directly for the programmes you provide, then possibly you have to define some system of accountability, but it is two different – totally different – sources of funding which will affect the programmes you hear.

Programmes are driven by the people who listen to them, and their perceived expectations. Now the independent sector in radio and next year in television is no longer obliged to operate under public service broadcasting considerations. In the olden days, 17 years ago or so when commercial radio was just starting you were obliged to spend 3% of your total net revenue on the employment of live musicians. Now there were ways and ways of getting round this. You could go out and blow the lot on a church service or a concert or a new jingle package, and within limits the IBA, that benevolent dictatorship, would wink or turn an eye But you were obliged at some point to employ local musicians. Now that actually gave local bands, new music, a fair crack at the airwaves, and they got it. An awful lot of local bands have broken on Radio Clyde, an awful lot have been broken on other radio stations. But that obligation no longer applies; it hasn't been monitored in the last 18 months and it no longer applies. You are no longer obliged to provide a mixture of programmes or to have your schedule approved, you're only obliged in radio to obey your promise of performance That means that you are obliged to keep to the sort of records you said you'd play and this is a business-like arrangement to make sure that you maintain the segment of the audience that you specifically bid for.

Radio can also be seen in business terms as a pattern for agglomeration. In two years you'll have to see what the open market does for television, when takeover time arrives. Well, takeover time is all the time in the wonderful of the wireless. We could get together today and we could go out and bid; Jimmy will give us the shopping list. Radio will narrow itself down to at the most six or seven groups of big businesses at the very most. Television will do the same. Look at radio for the pattern of change: Jimmy now controls most of Scotland, there are two little radio stations swimming out there somewhere in little pools. I see Radio Clyde like an amoeba swimming through the sea of life, and Radio Clyde, the great benevolent amoeba of radio is doing that all over Scotland. And of course in other parts of the world. Radio Clyde has stepped in to rescue the incremental station in Birmingham. Radio Clyde's interest extends, I stress benevolently, beyond the boundaries of the North West corner of Glasgow.

The whole radio market and, for that matter, the whole television market can't expand unless you reduce the BBC's share. The BBC enjoys the affections of about two thirds in radio, say for the sake of argument, 50% radio and television. 50% of people choose to have their broadcasting without commercials, give or take the odd flash for the Radio Times. Now what everybody needs is a bit of the BBC's share. Even in the top end of the market, half the people prefer to take their pop radio without commercials.

So, is the BBC range of radio programmes and programming safe? Only as long as the licence fee is safe. Forget subscription, it wouldn't even work for schools and education programmes. I really don't think subscription is on for radio. It does remain as *The Economist* rightly pointed out, a tricky problem, one that everyone wants to forget about.

We have at the moment a Director-General who is favourable to radio; we have a managing director of network radio, David Hatch, who is the best advocate of the wireless inside as well as outside of the BBC that we've seen in many a long year. Those of you who have worked for the BBC will well remember when there were three managing directors of radio in less than that number of years, and the ink was no faster dry on the doors than it had to be all scraped off again. Those people came and went back to television and left low morale behind at Broadcasting House. In the last five years or so, morale has really conspicuously been raised. Radio is no longer the shed at the back of the BBC's palace.

There is nothing like BBC radio on the air. There really isn't. ILR can't do as much for new bands as Radio 1, because independent radio stations are bound by the expectations of their audience. They are bound by narrow formats, and they don't tend to exceed them. In America this has now become a real real problem. Where do you get exposure for new music? Well on Radio 1 you still have it. No one does comedy and features like Radio 2. I really can't let Jimmy Gordon get away with the notion that Radio 3 is patronising and stuffy. The debt the arts in this country as a whole owe to Radio 3 is considerable. You will wait a long time to hear a new Tom Stoppard play in independent national radio. Radio 4 may have its stuffy moments, but even the mighty Thames TV, *pace* Roger Bolton, offers nothing like Radio 4 along the total range of achievements and programme. I am a keen listener to Radio 5, me and four other people, and I can tell when a programme is independently produced, it does not on the whole yet sound as good. I can get along without Channel 4's breakfast show, I can get along mostly without TV-am, and I can get along without all the radio stations that go "che tum tum tum, che tum tum tum". British culture as a whole as everyone agrees would be far poorer without BBC radio as it is now.

I am worried most of all by sponsorship. Everyone so far in this Symposium has brushed sponsorship aside and said oh, it will never amount to more than 10% of this, 10% of that. But why do people want to sponsor programmes as opposed to buying spot advertising? They get a hell of a lot more for their bucks out of it, that's why. I do not think the Proms would be anything like the Proms, were they to be the British Airways Proms. I do not think that the Sony BBC Symphony Orchestra would have quite the same ring to it as the BBC Symphony Orchestra. It is only a possibility. You dial up and down independent radio and every sports programme is sponsored, every single sports programme. Now that is the sort of programming you think they would be doing anyway. The audience must like it; it must be there because it's popular, but it's only there now because it is sponsored.

I think it would be a terrible irony if the BBC offered the government the daggers with which to stab it by its over- commercialism, its use of sponsorship and its somewhat intemperate rush to embrace broad commercial realities. Why has the government got to set the licence fee? Why can't the BBC have a rapport with its own consumers, with its own listeners and viewers, by setting its own licence fee? Why has it got to go cap in hand to the government and be awarded this as some kind of political favour? It is high time someone challenged that. I'm encouraged that there will be joint research, I'm encouraged that radio has achieved its own place in the sun after all this long time. I just hope to God it can stay there.

. . .

In the discussion, the following were among the points made:

Just as there were a hundred words for "rice" in Chinese, there were at least 92 different definitions of "community". There was powerful evidence that there was a demand for narrow definitions of music service, such as adult contemporary rock.

Michael Green was asked whether the new promiscuity he had detected among radio listeners was located in any particular age group, and he replied that most of the radio channel-switching was going on among the under-35s. The result was that broadcasters had to work harder to retain audiences, but it also gave radio stations the opportunity to experiment with programme forms.

A representative of the broadcasting unions underlined Gillian Reynolds's point that good talk radio cost money, and went on to say that all good radio cost money. But BBC radio was introducing independent producers to the network airwaves, even though there was no statutory reason to do so. Radio 5, where much of the new independent production was to be heard, seemed to be a problem for the BBC – it was underfunded and it sounded underfunded. Michael Green replied that even Radio 5 was only taking a couple of series per quarter from the independent sector, but that he welcomed the prospect of letting people who wanted to make good radio in the independent sector find a home on the BBC.

Another speaker asked Gillian Reynolds why she was so strongly opposed to sponsorship when (in the speaker's view) it was such a good way of funding speech programming. Gillian Reynolds was adamant that the real problem was one of editorial control.

A participant who worked for Community Service Volunteers recounted his experience with setting up two major sponsorship deals for BBC local radio, one with East Midlands Electricity and the other with Severn Trent Water, and he emphasized that there was no question at any time of them having or wanting editorial control. The speaker added that he was sure he could fund the whole of BBC Radio 4 by sponsorship without any difficulty.

Finally, the issue of serving narrow communities of interest on a nationwide basis was addressed. Given that it was impossible on a local basis to support, say, a jazz station or a classical station employing its own symphony orchestra, the suggestion was that digital radio by satellite was an excellent medium for these narrower interests.

Among those contributing to the discussion were:

Luke Crawley, BECTU
David Hallan, Community Service Volunteers
Jocelyn Hay, Voice of the Listener
Barbara Hosking, Yorkshire TV
Bevan Jones, freelance researcher

6 "The Baghdad Broadcasting Corporation"? How television dealt with the Gulf war

Geoffrey Dickens
MP (Conservative, Saddleworth)

John Eldridge
Professor of Sociology, University of Glasgow

Glyn Mathias
Controller of Public Affairs, ITN

Clive Ferguson
News producer, BBC Television

Chair: Graham Murdock
Senior Lecturer in Sociology, University of Loughborough
Producer: Charles Tremayne, *Granada Television*

Graham Murdock: Although this session is a late addition to the programme, there is no gap at all; the subject matter is absolutely central to the core theme of this conference. It is part of the crucial debate about the proper role of broadcasting in a democratic society, and its obligations towards on the one hand the government and on the other the citizen.

This is a debate about how broadcasters should position themselves in relationship to conflict. There is one position that says that if a decision to fight is made democratically then the primary responsibility of the broadcasters is to throw their weight behind that effort and to do nothing to impede it and everything to enhance it. This is the position not only of politicians, as you might expect, but also of some journalists.

The counter-position to that is of course the notion that broadcasting should be in some sense a public service and a public space, that its primary duty is to the citizen, and its duty is to provide the broadest possible range of disinterested information and to question the rationale or rationalization completely, even if those questions prove embarrassing. We can see both of those positions being played very clearly in the discussion about the Gulf conflict.

There are issues that are interesting about the Gulf conflict – broader issues about the future of news coverage and generally in light of comment about the crisis. There are two that I would particularly like to signal, which can be picked up presently. One has to do with the new visual technology of news and its relationship to public understanding; is it the case that computer graphics and the amazing advances in technology are likely to enhance public understanding or are they likely to inhibit it? The second issue has to do with the arrival of 24-hour-a-day news coverage and the particular case of CNN as a possible paradigm of the future and whether this kind of news set-up is likely to contribute to public understanding or not.

[The next speech begins after a clip of the ITN coverage of the "bunker" bombing.]

Glyn Mathias: I would like to make some specific comments about that tape in a minute but first I should just like to go back and set the scene very briefly about the way we tackled coverage of the war and the principles we tried to adopt.

We felt very strongly that we had to draw up our own guidelines about our coverage. We felt that whatever the Ministry of Defence might say, whatever the Government might say, we are responsible for our own output, we are independent broadcasters and we had to draw up our own guidelines. I helped to draw those up, and I shall just give you the headline which I think summarizes it, and it was this: that we had a duty to report as fully and as accurately as possible the events of the war but, at the same time, we would not broadcast information which carried any risk to the lives of allied personnel or jeopardized any allied operations. Now there are constraints in there on total freedom of reporting, they are constraints which we imposed upon ourselves. It was put to me very graphically by one of the reporters who returned from Saudi Arabia, Alastair Stuart, only a few days ago. "Look," he said, "we were talking to troops and soldiers and airmen who we knew in a day, or two days, a week, a month might be going out to die and we had always to be conscious of that fact." And that is a self-imposed restraint on the kind of coverage we could do.

It's extraordinary, however, how much information we did get out in this war; it was the first war in which satellite technology came right into its own. There were twelve ground stations in the Saudi war zone altogether amongst the various broadcasters, some right up at the front. The forward transmission units, at the divisional head-quarters of the First Armoured Division for instance, were bringing pictures back once, twice, possibly even three times a day right from the front line – an extraordinary technical achievement.

We also had extraordinary access which I don't think has ever been had in war time before. Remember those pictures of those pilots coming out of their aircraft in Bahrain and describing what it was like to fly those bombing sorties over Baghdad. They were extraordinary interviews, emotional interviews and I can't recall that ever having happened before.

Much has been made of the pooling system, the media response team pooling systems in Saudi Arabia where broadcasters were allocated to various parts of the British Forces. There was a similar American system. The television pictures which ITN got out from Paul Davies with one of the brigades were available to the BBC and other broadcasters. This pooling system carried with it various restrictions on what we could say. We had to agree not to disclose, for instance, the whereabouts of the brigade and that turned out to be crucial, of course, because of the element of deception that was critical to the allied attack.

We supplemented that participation in the pooling system with independent freelance efforts. We were able to range independently around the war zone – not as independently as we would have liked but, for instance, Peter Sharp produced an excellent report on the oil slick off the Saudi coast which he found when he was travelling near Khaffgi. He was travelling independently at the time and that was outside any controls and outside the pooling system. Sandy Gall, who brought back the first pictures of the ground attack into Kuwait, went in with the Saudis. He went in independently; he just slept up near the border that night and followed the Saudi tanks in. That was an independent operation, free of the controls and constraints except those which I have described which we imposed upon ourselves.

It was a multi-national war so many constraints, limitations and restrictions imposed by the allied military authorities could be got around and supplemented by information from a number of different sources. There were sources from other Arab countries and there were sources from the United States which were not, necessarily, official sources. It is sometimes forgotten that in this war Britain's contribution was only 6% of the allied effort. The number of other allied sources added to the information which was available and, in particular, one source was also important to us and that was the ability to report from Baghdad, which brings me back to the video you have just seen.

We felt that to be able to report the war fairly and accurately we had to include reports from Baghdad. It was a vital part of the jigsaw. Eye-witness journalism is an essential part of what television is about and it was far better to have our own team there, able to report what they saw, and not rely on second-hand reports from other sources.

It was not the case that if we went home there would be no reports out of Baghdad. It would merely have meant that we would have had to take second or third hand reports from other agencies if we weren't there. And that eye-witness journalism was crucial. I would like just to analyse very briefly the way Brent Sadler reported that horrific incident – and, by the way, I can't tell you how difficult it is to do that kind of report in the scenes of emotional horror which he was experiencing. You have to be a very experienced and, dare I say it, fairly hardened reporter to be able to report like that at scenes like that when they're in front of your eyes.

We did two things which were critical in that report. One was that Sadler made no judgement himself as to whether or not it was a civilian or military bunker. What you heard was the Iraqis claiming that it was a civilian shelter and not a military bunker. He also repeated the fact that the allies were claiming that it was a military target. He said what he saw, or what he couldn't see, and he didn't make any judgement. In fact on the following day he went back again to the site and reported other aspects of it which he couldn't see on the first day, such as camouflage paint and an aerial, which were indications that it might have been a military bunker.

Also surrounding that report we carried the allied version of events, so you can't see that report just in isolation. But also you may have noticed that, despite all the casualties, you didn't actually see any of the charred bodies. That is another sensitive decision we had to take on grounds of taste and decency (I see Colin Shaw in the audience there); we chose not to show the charred bodies. You saw the bodies covered with blankets. That is a difficult decision but the bodies were so horrific that we felt the audience would be too horrified by that. It was a horrific enough story anyway; the story was adequately told as it was.

So we felt we were justified in being there. That story was a justification in itself for being there. I would just add that in advance of every report from Baghdad, we always said that reports from Iraq were subject to Iraqi censorship. In every single story from Baghdad we made that absolutely clear, and it was our belief that if you tell the viewers the conditions under which they are receiving the information, they can make up their own minds. They can make their own judgements, and you can trust the viewer to do that.

Clive Ferguson: I would like to echo from the BBC's point of view that we made our decisions as well in terms of guidelines and taste. We had the likes of Brian Barron, Martin Bell and Kate Adie as our front line reporters. But although they are vastly experienced and have reported on events from all over the world in very difficult and often harrowing situations, even they were briefed on the sort of things that we were expecting from them. That mainly covered the tone of the reporting, sensitivity to the people back home, saying that we were very conscious of the possible casualties, and we are all thankful, of course, that there weren't very many. So there were a lot of problems which we anticipated which we, in fact, didn't have to deal with. But even those three very experienced front-line reporters were reminded of the sort of tone that was expected of them so that we were reflecting people's sensitivities, but not at the expense of reporting the story.

If I can talk about the operation in Saudi Arabia, we were operating from one of the most closed countries in the world. Long before the war they had their own restrictions. They let in, on average, 20 journalists a year and they were suddenly coping with about fifteen hundred journalists – journalists with voracious appetites. The American networks included CNN, who were broadcasting 24 hours a day every snippet of information within seconds of it being gathered by the various news teams. The visa restrictions on us getting into the country from the British point of view made life very difficult for us. It was to a certain degree rather more difficult for us than it was for ITN because it was the BBC engineers who were responsible for the dish that actually fed the pictures back from Paul Davies, Martin Bell, Kate Adie, and Robert Moore's reports from First Armoured Division. The BBC engineers also ran the satellite dish that fed back the pool reports and, indeed, unilateral reports for all the other UK broadcasters. Although those engineers were BBC employees they were working for everybody, but we found ourselves with about ten fewer people to go off on freelance operations. We still did them but, in common with ITN, on the occasions when we were found out it was harder for us. Peter Sharp lost his accreditation on the way back from Khaffgi – we lost ours on the way there, and somebody threatened to throw us all out of the country, not just the people who had lost their accreditation.

So there was a very difficult decision to be made on a daily basis as to when you took the risk of going out again. Sandy Gall, from memory, was arrested by the Saudis three times; Brian Barron was arrested twice and his cameraman had a stick in his cheekbone from the Saudi military because we were operating outside their guidelines.

In common with ITN, we didn't want to be restricted to doing just what the Saudis, or indeed what the British military or the American military, wanted us to do. When we tried to get up to the fighting in Khaffgi when the Iraqis actually came across the border, much to everyone's astonishment, there was a freelance operation. A French film crew actually got some of the best pictures and were able to provide them to the rest of us so that we could tell a better story than just the official combat pool pictures. They were spotted on the road and an American television reporter said "Hey, they're not members of the combat pool. Arrest them." So when you get your own journalists acting against you in such situations, it doesn't make life easy.

At the time of the Baghdad bunker or shelter, depending on which terminology you prefer to use, part of the outcry was that the BBC and ITN were not doing enough to highlight the atrocities that had happened in Kuwait; that there wasn't enough balance there. That did cause the broadcasters problems because the Iraqis, I think, took a CNN team to one hospital in Kuwait which demonstrated that everything was working just fine. We had no evidence, other than anecdotal evidence from Kuwaitis who were talking both in London and in Saudi Arabia about what had happened there. As with everything else that we were being told by the American military, by the Saudi military, by the British military, we maintained a fair degree of fairly healthy scepticism because our experience when we got to Kuwait was that if we had blindly reported all the stories that we were being told about the atrocities that had happened without any caveats, we would have been guilty of the grossest misinformation because, quite plainly, some of the reports were highly exaggerated. A lot of the things that people said didn't happen. On the simplest level, you may remember that one of the earliest reports was that the Iraqis had taken all the traffic lights in Kuwait City to Baghdad. They hadn't. It was reported that they were ripping up the paving stones along the newly paved corniche. They hadn't. So the degree of scepticism about all our reporting was very necessary

By and large, we would have liked a lot more freedom to broadcast and to roam about but constantly uppermost in our minds was that we were going to war and that people were possibly going to die. We were being warned by the military that it could be in very great numbers. For that reason we fell into line, to a certain degree, with some of their restrictions while trying to do our own thing but always bearing in mind that we were operating under our own guidelines, most of which, I think, worked as well as we could have expected them to.

Geoffrey Dickens: I ought to start by saying that I think all of us in this room would agree that the war correspondents were amongst some of the bravest people, and always have been over years of history. War correspondents go where others fear to tread and they do a very brave job, there's no doubt about that. However, what we have to consider is what is propaganda and psychological warfare. The aim during wartime is to gain world sympathy and, in the case of Iraq, to gain Arab sympathy, there's no doubt about that; to demoralize the coalition forces and to motivate their own troops by misinformation. This is what they tried to do. Because remember, whatever goes out on ITN or the BBC in this country is relayed through the Iraq Embassy, back to Baghdad so they see everything that is pouring out to the British public.

Propaganda works in all sorts of ways depending on how you think. The character assassination of Margaret Thatcher over the years got rid of Margaret Thatcher in the end because they almost presented her as an old witch on a broomstick. Poll tax – it was the community charge but they started to call it the poll tax and said so a number of times so that, in the end, everybody calls it the poll tax, so they won the propaganda war on that.

During the Second World War in Japan they had a young lady called Tokyo Rose who used to broadcast regularly. Certainly these broadcasts were taking place. We had Lord Haw Haw broadcasting to the nation which demoralized workers working in munition factories at home and their loved ones away fighting. It is just the same if Manchester United or Manchester City win at the weekend all the workers locally do a better job because they all feel better. You try to get underneath a nation, underneath its skin with propaganda warfare then you start to bite a bit. I felt that bunker scene was a bit like Doctor Goebbels going around in Berlin to hospital during the Second World War and showing people that have been injured. It made me sick seeing it all again, because I felt we fell into a trap.

But broadcasting has been used in many sophisticated ways. I'll go back to the Second World War. Then the enemy wanted to know if their V1 rockets were landing in the right place. So they found out that at the Albert Hall there was a live orchestral concert on a particular night. They listened in to that broadcast at the Albert Hall and if they heard the bombs going off in the background, they knew their range was right.

We were in the propaganda war in the Gulf, too. If you remember there were lots of shots of our helicopters taking out gunboats along the Gulf coast and our mine-sweepers taking out mines, clearly giving the impression that we were coming inland to attack, instead of which we did the long snake right round the back with the Eighth Army and others of the Tank Corps. And so we were putting misinformation out the same as everybody else. It was a glorified propaganda war both ways.

But you see television people can't have it both ways, can they? I don't blame the reporters, they've got to film everything they can get hold of, file it back to the UK and it's those selecting the items for the actual news bulletins that are the people I blame. As I say, they can't have it two ways because you can't on the one hand say to advertisers if you take a 15-second spot on our channel at so-and-so cost, our media research experts tell us you will probably sell x number of million pounds of your product, and yet try and distance themselves from the impact of propaganda sold back to the British people by the bad selection of film footage and propaganda fed out to us by an enemy.

In the past we never had television going into the home. The world is much smaller today. We ought to remind people the world is smaller because of television which was a British design. So communications are far superior and therefore we have a special duty to be very careful what we put into people's homes. As I said before, if the impact of commercials can sell products like that, the impact into our homes can be quite penetrating.

When I saw that film clip it made us look a bit barbaric. Well I know war is barbaric, we all know that and we could do without it. But, at the same time, we weren't shown around the injured and tortured and raped Kuwaiti population. We weren't shown the Amnesty International's report on what was happening out in Kuwait – the terrible atrocities to those people – and we weren't reminded many times that our Tornado pilots really won the war from the air. These Tornado pilots, in the early part of the war, flew low with great deliberation to be accurate with their bombs to cut down civil accidents on the civil population.

Yet, of course, to show a film like we've just seen tonight into our homes is to suggest that we almost went after a shelter. Do we know it was a shelter? It was never conclusively shown it was a shelter. And so why was that item even selected to be shown to us? It was just running our nation down, making us look quite barbaric not restoring the balance. And I felt it also brought into question the integrity of journalists because to take it in one direction and not to restore the balance, was one thing. I really think that would have been better not shown because it is one of the great accidents of war. Sadly war always produces its accidents and that it is the sad thing about it.

I wasn't on my own at the time. There were quite a few hundred people who got in touch with both ITN and the BBC. The nation at the time seemed outraged, saying "We are being used by Saddam Hussein and his advisers in his propaganda war. This is dreadful stuff to be showing on British television." And I think it was. I don't say anything about those reporters out there feeding stuff back. The people back at home had to make decisions. I suppose I honestly could be convinced that everything was done and it was done properly. I remain to be convinced. I haven't come here with such fixed views. But all I know is the first impact of seeing that – I thought, my God, we're being used, our television channels are being used for propaganda during a war, and this is serious, this is awful. That was my first reaction. Many letters followed. Many of my colleagues in the House felt the same. I thought it was a great shame on the integrity of journalism and I remain to be convinced otherwise.

Glyn Mathias: I think we fully understood the strength of feeling on this point. Perhaps there were a number of people in the BBC who did feel very strongly on this issue. Television brought the war home into people's living rooms. Up to then it had been something of an unreal war. We'd had pictures of pilots taking off with pictures of pilots coming back. But up to that point I don't think we had really seen any dead bodies. I don't think we had seen the casualties of the bombing. As I said, it had been a little unreal. And the first time during the war the pictures of the bombing did reveal the casualties.

Misinformation, we know, was used by both sides. You will remember the videos of the laser guided bombing and our emphasis on how accurate they were with cameras in the noses of the bombs and showing zeroing in on targets. I have subsequently been told by correspondents of Channel 4 News that something like 10% of the bombs that the allied dropped were actually so-called smart bombs and 90% were free-fall bombs. You have to remember that we were carpet bombing large chunks of Northern Kuwait and that the laser guided bombs were only a very small fraction of the bombing we did. Despite all that it would appear that the number of Iraqi casualties, at least according to claims that they made, was not that great, if you take into consideration the scale of the bombing. But these were the first pictures of casualties and it did make people realize that this war was for real, it wasn't boys at war with lots of technology. It was a serious war with people being killed and that was the reason for the numbers of people being at upset at these pictures coming into their living rooms. But it's not our fault. We didn't completely sanitize the war and pretend there were no casualties. War does have nasty results. People do die in wars. We have to take difficult judgements about what we show. I could not possibly tell you that we should go so far as to pretend it didn't happen.

Clive Ferguson: I agree. Reports on the bombing took fierce criticism. And we did ask very rigorously whether it was a shelter or not. I saw it the following day during a telephone interview with our reporter in Baghdad when he was being asked by Martin Lewis – was this, or was this not a command and control bunker? He said, "I can only tell you what I saw with my own eyes," which is all you can expect him to do. He also said "I've seen through what I think is 70% of the bunker. I don't know if I have seen it all." Now I think there is a growing feeling since that time that the American intelligence system actually came a cropper, that they got it wrong. But, nevertheless, that is not conclusive; that is the growing feeling and suspicion.

Professor John Eldridge: I have to say that I find it difficult to talk about this. Since I am a critic of the concept of objectivity, I think it is only fair to put it on the record at the outset that I was opposed to this war. My view was that the way of settling an extremely difficult issue was through the means of diplomacy and sanctions. Nothing that has happened since has caused me to change my mind.

Clearly it was a media-saturated war. It was an electronic war, both in terms of the weapons and technology and in terms of the media technology as well. I want to use some of the material that you will have seen as a basis for comment. This is absolutely not intended as some kind of attack on journalists as a category or as a profession. I am very conscious, not least as an academic well removed from the fray, of the courage and the tenacity which those journalists showed in most difficult circumstances.

There are important issues to be explored here. We need to remember the context within which the reporting of war takes place: the context of censorship, of disinformation, of black propaganda, of controlled briefings, of pooled reporting arrangements and so on.

And now there is the technology, the amazing technology of the communications systems. But at least we can distinguish fact from fiction, can't we? Well, can we? Deception is in the air. That is the nature of the situation which war engenders and we have heard the cliche about the first casualty so often we don't even need to complete the sentence.

What I want to do now is to take a group of video clips and explain what they are about.

The first group really has to do with what we might call "instant news." Primarily it's about CNN. You may remember that when war was declared, from a news flash, broadcasters here switched very quickly indeed to CNN. This was the new special ingredient – this 24-hour news programme used and watched by the powerful and also becoming a spectacle for the rest of us. Very soon CNN comes into play. What we are going to see now is first of all part of the clip from the Jerusalem sequence – this was on 17th January – and there will then be a brief comment taken from *The Late Show* about CNN. We will go back to the 17th where we will see an NBC broadcast and that is brought in because in the Late Show there is an NBC comment about CNN which is slightly dismissive, and you will also see that there is a problem of accuracy about the NBC report. And finally in this sequence we will see, very briefly, Charles Wheeler who is a veteran reporter whose scepticism I truly admire, and we have a few words from Charles Wheeler, only a few words but I think they are worth a large number of pictures. What you will see here is that the reporter has actually become the story and you might ask yourself a few questions about objectivity and the way in which information flows.

[Clip is shown]

You saw there the icon of the gas-mask, you saw some confusion, some panic, muffled voices and noises. What could they have known apart from their immediate experience? They became in large measure their own story. The sheer speed of the communications technology has eroded our capacity to reflect, interpret, sift. The imperative is to get the story on the air no matter how dubious or uncorroborated it is.

So the issue of instant news is a very serious one and needs to be addressed. It seemed to me that the voice of Charles Wheeler, an older voice and a mature voice and one who has a lot to go on, is a voice that we need to hear. It is the voice of scepticism. It's the voice of "wait and see," it is the voice of sift the evidence, it is the voice of making careful judgements and not making claims that cannot be substantiated.

Let us turn now to a second issue which stars David Dimbleby, the well known anchor person for the BBC. Here there are two facets of David Dimbleby; I don't intend this in an unduly critical way although maybe there is a slight edge in what I have to say. First there is what might be called "star-spangled Dimbleby" which is when he is absorbed with the weapons and the laser-guided missiles and he's so interested and fascinated by it that he actually asks to see it again. And having seen that he then goes into a little interview with Mr Cato, the American Ambassador to Britain, in which the issue of technology and its wonders and its precision and its accuracy is turned into a political matter: surely with weapons as accurate and as wonderful as this, the Americans will have the role in the world as the peace-keepers, not least in the Middle East, won't they? So we move from the possession of technology and all its incredible claims and capacities to the question of politics. That's what we see David Dimbleby doing.

[Clip is shown]

So we have the celebration of technology as accurate and surgical. We do not know, at that time, how accurate. We are in a kind of hall of mirrors between television technology and military technology, courtesy of the videos [taken from cameras in the nose-cones of laser-guided missiles – Eds.]. But, of course, while technology is the abstraction, the people are missing. Later on David Dimbleby in another sequence of this kind reminds himself and us that as that explosion takes place within the building there are people being killed. But, of course, you don't see them. And then we recognize, too, that we are in the business of interpretation. From technology to politics, we derive a right to rule based on surgical strike capacity. That is what that interview was about.

Now we come to Dimbleby the incipient Pilger, where he is getting a little concerned about the management of public opinion – what I would call "mood management." You will see an interview with a reporters, Mr Mandell, outside Downing Street, and you will also see another one which I decided to keep in from Paris from Nicholas Walter on the 23rd. This is a few days later. Here I want you to notice the body language – the way in which David Dimbleby uses his arm. We see him moving into a tirade which he realizes is getting a little tricky. As he moves into this tirade he gradually starts to try to pull himself out again because he's in a rather tricky area. I think John Pilger would be more at home with it.

[Clip is shown]

That was a very important sequence and I ran it at some length because it draws to our attention the issues of news management and the way in which public opinion in itself can be manipulated. Now we cannot know whether all that success which was attributed to President Mitterand [in the clip] is really down to him, but certainly it is a very important point to bear in mind. What we notice about David Dimbleby is a whole interpretative activity. He refers to "rational people", sensible people who watch the BBC and other such things who know how to handle themselves in these matters. And then he says we're sceptical about things that we shouldn't be sceptical about. In other words, we are being let down somewhere. There's all this tremendous unease about it. What this leads me to say is that the sceptical attitude is really what I want to advocate. And it's not the same as objectivity. A sceptical attitude is the questioning, doubting attitude which fully recognizes the context of deception and misinformation as well as the positive attempts which are made to influence public opinion.

Whether or not what is going on is true or accurate, the issue which seems to be at stake half the time is the question of the public mood and that's very important.

We've come to the last section where we going to talk about the victims. Here there's a brief piece from Brent Sadler on Cruise missiles on 1st February. And then, secondly, we have a clip from the BBC on the 14th about the Baghdad bombing, the day after when we see Peter Sissons questioning Jeremy Bowen. We see the actual interview. Then we see the bombing of the convoy and, last of all, a short excerpt from the Late Show on 7th March dealing with the *Observer* photograph of the charred body of the man in the vehicle.

I really want to defend both ITN and the BBC in the way in which, in general terms, they handled the situation in Baghdad. Just to give one quotation which typifies the way it was done from ITN, we hear "the latest pictures to come out of Iraq show extensive damage caused, the Iraqis say, by allied bombers. This is an image of life in Iraq that Saddam Hussein is anxious for the world to see and believe. The pictures were supplied by the Ministry of Information as propaganda. They graphically illustrate the suffering. The pictures are being used as a weapon as a means to influence world opinion. The fact that Iraq supplied the material draws natural suspicions about its authenticity. These people are claimed by Iraq to be recent victims of the bombing but they have not been independently verified as such." If you read *Index on Censorship* for this year you will also read a very significant article by John Simpson about the experience of reporting in Baghdad, which I commend to you.

[Clip is shown]

So, when technology comes down to earth it finds its victims.

. . .

In the discussion which followed, Dr David Morrison, Research Director of the Institute of Communications Studies at the University of Leeds, described a research programme mounted at Leeds in which a massive national survey was combined with data collected in twelve discussion groups. In the discussion groups, unedited footage from the BBC, ITN and, in some cases, European broadcasters (which had not been shown in the UK) was used as the basis for discussion about issues such as how much explicit violence in war coverage was acceptable. The research would be published later in 1991.

Another speaker, addressing the issues of "instant news" covered during the session, put forward the argument that there was too much continuous coverage of the war on television, and reported that many people, inside and outside the industry, had made this point. Shorter hours of coverage would have encouraged broadcasters to apply more rigorous analysis and consideration to what was being shown.

In that context, it was also argued from the floor that radio was able to provide more useful analysis than television. Despite the fact that this session had been subtitled "how television covered the Gulf war", the achievement of Radio 4 News FM was worthy of note; unencumbered by the need to show pictures, Radio 4 News FM had been able to combine expert analysis *in extenso* with raw information (such as the live daily military briefings) where required.

Among those who contributed to the discussion were:

Andrew Curry, independent producer
John Gray, independent consultant
Dr David Morrison, University of Leeds
Hanna Pout, Bar Ilan University

7   "I'm Glad You Asked Me That": The political interview

Glenwyn Benson
Editor, On The Record, BBC Television

Max Atkinson
Communications consultant

Matthew Parris
Journalist and broadcaster

Chair: Sue Elliott
Independent Television Commission

[The session started with a compilation of historical interview clips, including a famous meeting between Robin Day and the then president of Egypt, Gamal Abdul Nasser]

Max Atkinson: I don't claim to know exactly how TV interviews work. If I did I would be a millionaire by now. However, I do have a long-standing interest in the workings of question and answer sequences, originally in the context of research in which I was involved in court rooms. There has also been a little bit of work done on news interviews as a phenomenon and I don't plan to bore you with any of that tonight other than for one little feature. I was told it was supposed to be light-hearted. So I am starting with a piece of video tape.

What I have to say is based on a small piece that I wrote in *The Independent* which was triggered by two interviews that Brian Walden did with Margaret Thatcher and Nigel Lawson just after Nigel Lawson's resignation. In particular it was triggered by a strong sense of shock on seeing Nigel Lawson actually answering the questions as put. In fact I remember at the time feeling that the interview was all over, bar the shouting, within five minutes and it was quite safe to go and have Sunday lunch. It was that astonishment at seeing a politician give straight answers to straight questions that really triggered my interest. So I have put together a compilation just to remind you of what happened.

[Clip follows: Brian Walden interviews Nigel Lawson]

That was the sort of thing that shocked me in the directness of the answers. And part of the shock was the incredible contrast between that and what we had seen in the previous episode of the saga, the interview with Mrs Thatcher herself. And I have got just the first exchange from that interview to give you a feel for the difference in the directness with which the questions were asked.

[Clip follows: Brian Walden interviews Margaret Thatcher]

That is a long way from being a very direct answer. It was also a long way from being short and succinct. In fact the overwhelming impression was that it was prepared, if not rehearsed. We had heard endlessly the previous week the repetition of the lines about "unassailable," about "ministers deciding and advisers advising".

I think the contrast between these two interviews highlights what I think is widely regarded as a problem with the current state of media interviews with politicians. Increasingly the interviewees have started to treat, questions as cues or prompts to make miniature speeches. And, in so doing, they seem to feel very little regard for having to be under any obligation to address the question as asked.

So I thought what I would do is just to look at one or two questions which I think are raised by this and then to suggest possible solution and invite other people to join in the suggestion of solutions, of alternative forms of television programming that might solve the problem.

First, where has the practice come from? The second question I want to address is, how effective is not answering the question from the point of view of its impact on viewers? And, thirdly, what, if anything, should we or can we do about it?

Where has it come from is perhaps the easiest part to answer. It has come from the burgeoning media training industry. The trouble with media training is that it presupposes that we know an awful lot about how question and answer sequences work and, in particular, how interviews work. The fact is we don't. And faced with this lack of knowledge, most trainers resort to a single piece of advice. And that is, decide what you are going to say and go in and say it irrespective of what the question was. This seems to be becoming the standard way in which people are groomed to appear on the media.

I am not against preparation but, in its crude form, as I just articulated, I am very sceptical about whether it's good advice or not.

And this brings me to the second question – of how effective it is in terms of the audience. My own view is that audiences just aren't that dumb, that they can see perfectly well what's going on. The fact of the matter is that people are very used to interpreting what people say and how they say it as a basis for deciding what kind of person the speaker is. This applies in conversation and it applies in any other situation. If being seen to evade questions is used in that way then the chances are that the politician will be seen as evasive, untrustworthy, shifty, even dishonest. I simply don't understand why it is they think that they can get away with it. I presume it is only because of the lack of knowledge about their immediate impact on people sitting in their living rooms that enables them to carry on with it.

From the point of view of the third question – what, if anything, should be done about the problem – I think this is, perhaps, the most intriguing part of the whole issue. I am suggesting that interviewees have been able to subvert or duck the normal conventions associated with question/answer sequences. When I say normal conventions, what I mean is that we all know, from a very stage, that when you hear a question, you should give an answer. What we have now is a situation where the relationship between answers and questions is usually tangential to say the least.

One could ask, if that's the case, if politicians are routinely doing that, why don't the interviewers do something about it? It is easier said than done for one very good reason which has to do with the available options for dealing with naughty people who won't answer questions. How, in other settings, are such people dealt with? For example, think about court hearings. One of the things that happens in court if you don't answer a question is that you get interrupted and told to answer the question. You may get interrupted by the opposing counsel objecting to what you are saying, in which case the judge will rule on whether or not what you are saying is correct or allowable. In any event, almost all the available options for dealing with speakers who don't answer questions have a hostile edge to them. They involve being aggressive in one way or another.

That raises the question of why, then, can't interviewers be more aggressive, more hostile, more combative in the interviews? The answer to that is a relatively simple one and it has to do with the fact that the borderline between hostility and bias is a very narrow one – if you start being hostile in trying to get somebody to answer the question, repeating the question, insisting that they answer it, it starts to look as though you are taking sides, it starts to look as though you have a political bias. Retention of some sense of political neutrality is part of the stock in trade of professional television interviewers. It is certainly interesting to see how very touchy Brian Redhead is when he is accused of political bias on the *Today* programme.

So interviewers are at present caught on the horns of this dilemma, that the interviewees – the politicians – are free to say what they like without regard for the normal conventions of question/answer sequences, but the interviewers are not free to do anything about it without putting their professional credibility on the line. If that's so, it might seem a rather pessimistic view, but we're doomed to listen to these extremely boring mini-speeches for ever more. We should be thinking about radical and creative alternatives in the form of programming. I'm going to leave you with one. I've been told that this is a somewhat facetious suggestion but I don't see why it couldn't work.

The scenario would be that one would have interviews taking place in a cock-pit, somewhat like *Question Time*, except that the function of the audience wouldn't be to answer questions; it would be to press buttons next to their seats which indicate the extent to which they feel the politician had answered the question. This would be fed into a thermometer at the back of the set which would rise according to the vote of the audience. If it failed to rise above a certain point then the interviewer would have special rights then to demand that the question be asked. This would seem to me to make for very good television. I doubt whether many politicians would agree to go on such programmes. That is an interesting issue because the question of at what stage the broadcasters can exert their power to determine what the programmes are like is central. Sooner or later the politicians would have to conform if they wanted the publicity – so long as we never have television advertising for politics in this country. But so long as we don't have television advertising it might be that the broadcasting companies could become tougher in the way that they establish the rules for the game.

Glenwyn Benson: Actually, *On the Record* is not exactly what you are talking about but we have done something quite similar. After the second leadership ballot, we did a programme with an audience where people had a little gadget in their hands; when a politician was speaking they could press a button one way or the other way, up or down. It raised an instant reaction to what the politician is saying. One of the problems with what you are suggesting is that people register in a negative way when they don't like the answer. And, for example, I remember this very clearly, when Douglas Hurd was asked about his policy on the poll tax, and he was defending it very articulately and very clearly and you could see exactly where he stood and he was answering the question, but the line was going really steeply down because these Tory waiverers did not agree with what Douglas Hurd was saying. So there might be a problem with that but it appeals to me in principle.

Sue asked me to say something about the relationship between politicians and the programmes. But first I would like to pick up partly on what Max said about evasiveness.

I think evasiveness is an art in its own right. It has been studied quite a lot. Lawson is exceptional. That was a very exceptional interview. But Lawson is one of the few politicians who does answer. There is a handful of them. I would think Gould is another very good example. Gould is very candid. Most of them are quite evasive. But they are very good at being evasive so you don't always notice. I mean you do if they are not skilled at it. But you don't always notice.

Thatcher and John Smith are particularly good at using aggression as a way of being evasive. Thatcher is excellent at pushing the interviewer on to the next subject by attacking him or her. She does it quite often. When she is doing BBC interviews she has often done it, if you study them, in terms of attacking the BBC – often over the exit poll in the last election. It has been charted by quite a lot of academics – the way in which people use aggression as a way of pushing the interviewer on, because the interviewer feels uncomfortable with this person being aggressive towards them.

Neil Kinnock has been studied in the way he uses evasion. He quite often uses it in a negative reply in order to evade. So he will tell you what the Labour Party will not be doing in response to a question. It's a bit more transparent, because the viewer can see that that's what he is doing. Another one some people are quite good at is that they throw the question back at the interviewer. Sometimes that is a bit risky. But it is an art and some people are quite successful. The people who are good at evading make you feel slightly uncomfortable but you're not really sure that it's because they are evading. All you know is that there has been some kind of nasty feel to the interview somehow. I think it is a pretty successful technique.

Anyway, just to go on. Sue wanted me to say briefly something about our relationship with politicians.

I'm sorry to disappoint but I've never come across politicians trying to censor beforehand what they would be asked about. We just don't find that. That maybe because the programme is live and it maybe because they get a long chunk in which to speak. The interview is usually about twenty minutes or even longer.

But in terms of our normal relationships with politicians, as long as you don't ask a politician something which is absolutely nothing to do with their portfolio, in other words you don't ask the social services minister about defence or something, in which case he could quite legitimately say "I'm sorry that's not my portfolio", I've never found that politicians won't speak even about the most sensitive subjects, once they've agreed to come on. For example, Geoffrey Howe came on just after Tienanmen Square when there was a row about Hong Kong. He had a live audience, via satellite, from Hong Kong and a live audience of British people. It was a very, very difficult situation for Geoffrey Howe because the audience from Hong Kong was incredibly hostile to him and what he was saying – the British audience were not terribly supportive either. But, having made the decision to come on, he was prepared to accept any questions that we threw at him.

I think the real problem is the sanction that they have which is that they may say "we won't come on". That is much more of a problem than them trying to fence with you about what they will or won't discuss. It is a very big sanction that politicians have. All one can be grateful for, as a programme editor is that they don't use it more than they do.

I would say in the interview that Walden had with Thatcher that particular weekend, they were very lucky they had booked that interview in a long time in advance – they booked it in the summer. I doubt very much whether the Prime Minister would have come on that weekend. I doubt it very much.

There are other examples that one could think of where politicians want to bury things and, therefore, they won't come on. My own observation about this is that the Labour Party are more likely to adopt the attitude of wanting to bury policy squabbles than the government are. But I think you can understand that because there is not the same need for the Labour Party to justify policy decisions with the public as there is for the government because their policy is not actually being inflicted on the public. They don't have to persuade, they don't have to win hearts and minds in order to govern the country because they are not governing the country. And so, obviously, it is very much in their interest to make sure that when they do come on, they do know what the policy is, they have decided that they are united on it. I can understand, therefore, although it's quite irritating from a programme maker's point of view, why you tend to get the Labour Party being more wary about coming on in times of crisis, or troubles in the government.

I am quite impressed, though, at the extent to which government ministers do come on when things get rough. The Foreign Secretary is a very good example from my experience. He came on our programme when Ridley resigned; the question to him, very embarrassing for him, was: "How can you continue to do your job because it is well known that the Prime Minister's views are exactly the same as Nicholas Ridley's?" The Foreign Secretary was prepared to come on that weekend and answer those questions. He went on *Walden* the weekend Howe resigned – again a very difficult and embarrassing situation for him. But he went on the television. Heseltine came on *On the Record* the weekend after the Budget and his own speech in the

Commons – a very difficult situation with nothing much for him to say, and yet he was prepared to come on.

There are quite a lot of examples which, to one's surprise, indicate that in our democracy Ministers still feel its their job to come on and put the message across. So I don't think one should be too depressed about that.

Sue Elliott: Matthew, what was your experience on *Weekend World*?

Matthew Parris: As a presenter of *Weekend World* I am only aware of one case when someone refused to come on and even then he didn't refuse; Neil Kinnock wanted to make conditions about an interview that I was to have with him – he didn't want more than x per cent of the interview to relate to defence. The programme very vigorously resisted his insistence and so the interview was scrapped. Later he did come on.

As Glenwyn says, other ministers or other politicians played it rather more cleverly. Mrs Thatcher simply refused ever to come on *Weekend World* for the two years when I was presenter – and did something, I think, to hasten the demise of *Weekend World* for that reason. They boxed cleverer than being so foolish as to try and make preliminary conditions. I don't think many people in television would accept that kind of thing. Word always gets round when people try to do that. It gets into the press one way or the other so just isn't worth trying.

By way of general comment I simply would like to say that I don't think any of this matters very much. I think that, as in the natural world, there is some levelling mechanism at work and always will be. As in the development of any competitive sport, when one party to the contest learns new techniques or new ways of defending himself or herself, the other party eventually develops corresponding or answering techniques whereupon the first party finds something to give them a temporary edge whereupon the other party finds something to change that edge.

When interviewing started as a political tool in the early days of broadcasting, it was considered a great courtesy if a politician agreed to give an interview at all. The interview was given in a very deferential manner. No questions were asked other than questions which it was assumed the Minister or politician would be prepared to handle, and if the politician, and this is a most important point, wished to say "no comment" or "that is not something about which I choose to answer", that was considered perfectly all right. That was not a defeat. It was not to the discredit of the man or woman that he gave that answer.

The ethos has changed. There's no longer an unwritten understanding as to what questions will and won't be asked. There's no longer any sort of deference. The idea that an interview is to seek for information has gone almost completely out of the window. I can't remember a *Weekend World* interview in my two years when I was genuinely looking for information. On the contrary we, the team, had decided what we thought the person ought to say if he or she was being honest and our aim was to persuade them to say it. There was no question of them knowing something that we didn't know and us wishing to enquire about it. That was not the spirit of the interview. So it's changed. Interviewers are not looking for information any more, they are trying to bludgeon things out of people and it's not surprising that politicians have learnt answering tactics; one of the best ones being the diversionary tactic. A politician is no longer allowed to say "no comment," "I won't answer that question it's not something I want to talk about." And so a politician talks about something else. If those of you who are media people were prepared to accept from a politician the answer "no comment" as an acceptable answer, and if the public were any longer prepared to accept "no comment" as an acceptable answer from politicians, I think you would find yourselves getting a lot straighter, quicker, shorter answers from politicians that you do. Much of what they say is just another way of saying "no comment".

We looked at those clips at the beginning. I took the side of the politician in almost every case. The case of the first one, was it the young Robin Day? I wasn't sure. But whoever the interviewer was he was asking a nonsensical question. He was asking Nasser to say whether he recognized the existence of Israel. And did the question mean "recognize Israel diplomatically"? No, because Nasser said quite clearly that he didn't. Did the question mean "recognize those people were physically there at that time"? Well, plainly, Nasser did because everybody knew that the Israelis were there at that time. So what was Nasser supposed to say? What sort of answer would have been an acceptable one? The reason that he wiped his brow was that it was hot and, had he not wiped his brow, that would be a sign that someone had taught him that it doesn't look good to wipe your brow. It wouldn't have been a sign that he was a particularly honest politician.

I think it is a point worth making in general terms that the honest man or woman is not necessarily the man or woman who has learnt to give apparently straight answers to straight questions. And the dishonest man or woman is not necessarily the man or woman who grows uncomfortable when confronted with direct questions and tends to give answers where one does better to read between the lines than to hear the answer direct. Sometimes a very honest man or woman doesn't answer in an apparently straight way. Sometimes a very dishonest man or woman knows how to answer in an extremely straight way. We are talking now about techniques. We are not talking about the human qualities of which those techniques are supposed to be but are not, in fact, the evidence.

Geoffrey Howe having resigned, you saw Kenneth Baker interviewed. Kenneth Baker's mistake was to give an interview in those circumstances. But there was plainly absolutely nothing he could say, the Party had temporarily anyway fallen flat on its face and he was not going to say that. No party chairman ever is going to say that.

Lawson versus Thatcher, yes. But Mrs Thatcher was Prime Minister. She has a lot to hide. Any Prime Minister does, or did. Nigel Lawson had nothing to lose. He had resigned. When you have got nothing to lose it's very easy to be honest and give short answers to questions.

As for pressing buttons when you don't approve of the answer that's being given or don't like the way the answer is going, far from encouraging the qualities of honesty or straightforwardness in politicians that will, in fact, be an advantage to the most odious kind of politician of all – the politician who senses what his audience wishes to hear and tailors his answers in that direction.

90

So I just see the whole thing as the jungle, the law of the jungle. Interviewers are up and at them, politicians defend themselves as best they can and both sides, I think, must use whatever weapons come to hand. And good luck to both sides.

. . .

In the discussion, the following were among the points made:

American politicians, it was pointed out, do not use evasive techniques in the same way that British politicians do, but their different approach to TV was coloured by the fact that it is possible to buy airtime for political advertising on American television.

But another speaker argued that there already was political advertising in Britain, and it came in the form of the political interview. Television journalists were being used by party machines to help create the imagemakers' wanted images of politicians. Using free editorial was cheaper than buying time, and the effect was that the audience was coming away with the image of the politician desired by that politician.

Against this it was said that it presupposed that the party managers were cleverer than they actually were. They had very little knowledge of the communications processes at work in television.

It was suggested from the floor that politicians' views of television were moulded as much by their experience of appearing on it as by watching the output. The story that Mrs Thatcher's determination to reform ITV began on the day that *Weekend World* sent 50 technicians to Downing Street to do a live two-handed interview was probably not apocryphal.

Things in Britain had changed, said another speaker, since the beginning of the televising of Parliament; Matthew Parris, himself a parliamentary sketch writer, added that the televising of Parliament had made it easier for sketch writers, because readers now had a real sense of what went on inside the Chamber.

Political interviews in Germany and France, noted a speaker, were much softer; British political interviewing was more adversarial because British politicals were more adversarial.

Participants' attention was drawn to *After Dark*, a programme which gives its participants enough time to "send themselves and the audience to sleep." Only two politicians had ever accepted an invitation to appear on it. The makers of *After Dark* concluded that anyone who was not capable of sustaining an act for two and a half hours was not going to wish to appear on it.

Among those contributing to the discussion were:

Rod Allen, Television Entertainment
Steven Barnett, Henley Centre
Bevan Jones, Freelance researcher
Jerry Kuehl, Open Media
Richard McAllister, University of Edinburgh
Gillian Reynolds, *Daily Telegraph*
Murray Weston, British Universities Film & Video Council

8　The Broadcasting Bill 1996: The Parliamentary Debate

Rod Allen
Chief executive, Television Entertainment Limited, London

It is a two-year-old "tradition" of the Symposium to hold one of its debates in the standing House of Commons set at Granada Television. The idea is that the Parliamentary form of debate – not often used in ordinary conference settings – can create new ways of looking at broadcasting policy issues, and the process can in some part usefully simulate the way in which policy issues are debated in the actual House of Commons. It also provides a good deal of fun, allowing participants to address one another as the Honourable This and That; giving some lucky people permission to dress up as Black Rod and Mr Speaker; and letting everyone gleefully imitate the extraordinary braying and clubland behaviour seen and heard on broadcast coverage of the House.

This year, the Symposium-as-House-of-Commons debated a bill drafted by Colin Shaw, director of the Broadcasting Standards Council, which had as its objective the breaking up of the BBC into separate radio, television and external broadcasting institutions. The Bill would have created a single body to collect licence revenue, which would distribute it about the three new organizations, and there would be a revolutionary plan to elect members of the board of governors – not by universal suffrage, but by suffrage among all those willing to pay a couple of quid to get on the voting rolls.

Since participants were invited to seat themselves on one side of the House or the other, thus indicating opposition to or agreement with the Bill, it seemed, at least superficially, that the idea was to divide participants into those who more or less supported the continued and unaltered existence of the BBC – the Opposition – and those who wished to do away with it altogether and replace it with a more market-oriented and less powerful public broadcasting structure – the Government.

What turned out in fact was that almost everybody on either side of the House wanted to change the BBC; but almost nobody wanted to do away with it. This very effectively illustrated a deep and troubling problem which faces the BBC as it prepares itself to do battle for the Charter and Licence in 1996.

Opening for the opposition, Steven Barnett declared that the BBC was not perfect. But it was a "national institution which is respected throughout the world". He referred to a Rowntree social attitudes survey which showed that the BBC came near to the top of a list of institutions admired by the public (and that Parliament came near to the bottom of the same list).

The degree of disquiet about the BBC among its supporters was emphasized when Shelley Lanchbury, a trades unionist, speaking from the opposition front bench, said that radical reorganization, including the prospect of elected governors, was actually the most exciting aspect of the Bill.

Independent producer Andrew Curry, also speaking as a supporter of the BBC (having disposed of the carefully-rehearsed phrase that "This Bill is a weasel designed as a camel") damned the BBC as the South Eastern Broadcasting Corporation, or "London Calling".

Colin Shaw, who drafted the Bill, spoke of "making the consumer sovereign", and destroying the "ancient system" of governors; but he was met with a strong and coherent response from Kim Peat, of Channel 4, again speaking from the side which supported the BBC. She said that the Bill gave broadcasters no remit for the regions, for women or for ethnic minorities. "What we want," she said, "is a truly accountable BBC. We want real elections for all the governors." This was a view that was reinforced by Sue Elliott, of the ITC, who said that the democratic imperative dictated that whole board of governors should be elected by the public, and that the Secretary of State should have no say in their election.

Alastair Burt, the only "real" MP to join in the debate, had his doubts about direct elections. Supporting the Bill, he joked that direct elections tended to send a "bunch of layabouts" to the House of Commons; they might create the same sort of problems for the BBC. He suggested a novel form of appointing governors by which a national game show might be held on television every so often to choose the right men and women. Gillian Reynolds, of *The Daily Telegraph*, however, complained that any attempt to change the way the governors are appointed ran the danger of swapping the great and the good for the small and the terrified.

In closing, however, Alastair Burt made the point that those who fear direct control of the BBC by the Government have been given serious problems as to suggesting an alternative by the lack of democratic accountability in today's environment.

It has been a very long time since the word "accountability" has popped up during a Manchester Symposium debate. It was Stuart Hood, in the sixties, who argued fiercely for accountability and access to the broadcasting institutions, and many Manchester Symposia throughout the seventies pursued this issue fiercely, until the eighties took over and issues of funding and structure became more fashionable.

For the BBC, the doubts with which its supporters support it must be a serious matter. There is still passion about the need for a large, public, non-commercial broadcasting institution. But from this debate it seems that the BBC is supported mainly because it is the only example of this structure that we have, and not because it has performed particularly valiantly in the duties of a public service broadcaster. The lurch towards the search for non-licence-fee income support which has been masterminded by director-general Michael Checkland with the help of BBC Enterprises' chief executive

James Arnold Baker has hopelessly compromised any argument about the licence fee being a "pure" form of funding which keeps the Corporation free from the taint of commercial motivation. The Wenham theory that the BBC should go for at least 50% of the available audience has done real damage to any argument that the raisons d'etre for maintaining the BBC through public funding are cultural and social – not least because there are huge acres of broadcasting time on BBC 1 (and sometimes BBC 2) during which it is impossible to find any kind of programme which might remotely be described as public service. BBC 1 on a Saturday evening is an extremely good example.

The Manchester debate suggests that the BBC might listen more closely to its best friends than to the decoded messages it gets about how best to please the politicians as it girds itself for the approach to 1996. It has been brilliantly successful in matters like industrial relations reform, and it is finally learning how to take the independent producer quota into account. But those who see the Corporation as being at the cultural centre of national life appear not to be convinced that it has learned the lesson of the past two decades. There is a need for accountability and access which goes beyond consumerism and modelling slavishly the whims of the latest Home Secretary.

9 "It's your BBC – now run it": the simulation exercise

Andrew Curry
Independent producer

"It's Your BBC – Now Run It" was a simulation exercise set in the near future, in which competing teams were required to run the BBC against a background of falling budgets and in an unsettled political environment. The exercise was designed to put groups in the position of evaluating services and programmes when they no longer had sufficient income to finance their existing range of services.

In January 1991, the trade magazine *Television Week* published the following report:

"**BBC staff to pay for pegged licence fee**

"The BBC is being told to increase its independent commissions and cut staff by 2,800 over the next three years to compensate for the government's decision to hold the licence fee to 3% below the rate of inflation.

"The recommendations are in a report from management consultancy Price Waterhouse.

"Michael Checkland, the BBC's Director-General, reacted to the pegged fee increase this week by announcing an immediate recruitment freeze in all central directorates, as well as the legal, engineering, corporate affairs, policy and planning departments. But he said cuts in programme quality would be resisted.

"The BBC had argued in talks with Government ministers that inflation in broadcasting was higher than in outside industries. But the ministers stuck by Price Waterhouse's findings that the BBC could survive by cutting costs and increasing revenue over the next five years."

(*Television Week*, 17-23 January 1991)

It was against this real-world background that the scenario for the simulation was constructed.

95

The Scenario

It is 1993. Prime Minister Major's Conservative government has a majority of two seats, and is trailing badly in the opinion polls. The companies in the Channel 3 system have benefited from the vigorous interpretation in the 1991 franchise round of the notion of the quality threshold, and have money to spend on programming. Channel 3 regularly achieves a 46% audience share.

Channel 4 continues to struggle at about 9%, while BSkyB now reaches 4 million homes, and is picking up about 6%. (Its share of viewing, in those homes which have it, is 25-30% – mostly for its two movie channels). Channel 5? Come back in 1996.

Against this background, the BBC is suffering. Its share hovers just below the 40% mark. The licence fee has continued to fall in real terms. The BBC Board of Management continues to review the scope of the Corporation's activities, but has not yet taken radical decisions about cutting services. 20% of the BBC's output is coming from the independent sector. There are continuing rumours that the government might be prepared to amend the Charter to allow it to take some advertising – but they are only rumours. What is known is that the government's view will be affected by the BBC's ability to compete, measured by audience share.

"It's Your BBC – Now Run It" unfolded over two principal sessions – each representing a year – and each group had to select its own strategy, balancing the conflicting requirements of popular programming, maintaining public service requirements, and finding additional sources of revenue.

Each group started the game with enough money to survive the first year: a licence fee payment for 1993 worth £3.75m. Of this, £1.3m was committed to other services (for example radio & regional services), and £2.3m was to run the network television system (of which £1.2m had been paid in advance to the workforce for programmes in the coming year). Each team also had a budget based on the BBC's real balance sheet; the numbers were different, but in proportion to the real thing. This budget, reproduced in the figure below, also gave the team clues about its competitors' financial position.

Subscription services were assumed (as in real life) to have a negligible impact on the organization, and the groups were also told that Independent National Radio was starting to make inroads on the radio services.

Using its allotted income, each group was asked to construct a schedule of 21 programmes representing, roughly, a typical week's mid-evening schedule.

The programmes were represented by playing cards, each card standing for an hour of programming. The different suits were different types of programming: Hearts were drama, Diamonds entertainment, Clubs factual programming, and Spades were bought-in programming. Any Jack, whatever its suit, was a news programme.

Audience share of each programme was represented by the value of its card, ten being the highest, and ace the lowest. What aces lacked in audience share they made up for by winning broadcasting awards.

96

The Budget

	£m		
The BBC			
Income, Year 1			
Licence fee	3.60		
Enterprises etc	0.15		
	3.75		

	£m		
Expenditure, Year 1			
Committed			
Regional television	0.40		
Network radio	0.60	of which:	£'000s
		Radio 1	75
		Radio 2	130
		Radio 3	125
		Radio 4	170
		Radio 5	100
Regional/local radio	1.30		
Available for network TV funding	2.45		
of which:			
staff costs	1.20		
cash	1.25		

Channel 3		
(10 programmes)	2.00	

Channel 4	1.00	
of which:		
general programmes	0.75	
drama fund (10 programmes)	0.25	

BSkyB	1.25	
of which:		
special programmes	1.00	
general programmes	0.25	

The amount to be paid for each of these programmes was strictly negotiable – in this game, everything was up for negotiation – but there were guide prices published on the walls, and these were in line with the latest available BBC figures, ranging from an hour of peak time drama at £600,000, to an hour of news at £90,000, to an hour of lower audience bought-in programming at £25,000.

This programming was available to the BBC from a number of sources:

(i)   its own workforce;
(ii) independent producers;
(iii) the international distribution market.

In addition the Board of Broadcasting Control from time to time announced auctions for special events, represented by Queens, Kings, and Jokers.

Before the start of the game, the groups were treated to speeches from politicians representing the major political parties outlining their favoured broadcasting policies. These people were participants in the simulation rather than real politicians, although sometimes it was hard to tell. The Conservative, already in power, was in favour of cost-effectiveness and encouraging the independent sector, and the Liberal Democrat wanted more women at management level. The Labour shadow minister spoke enthusiastically of community radio (surprisingly, this become a factor in the game) before unveiling a startling programme: among other things, pensioners and claim-ants were to be exempt from the licence fee, and this to be paid for by nationalising a range of popular magazines, including *Smash Hits*, *Jackie Q*, and no doubt *Kerrang!* as well.

With that, the groups were off – with one final inducement. Any group which was prepared to put real money, in pounds sterling, on the table, up to a maximum of £2 per head, would have it exchanged into the "Bank of Broadcasting Credit" scrip which had been specially printed for the game. This was such an attractive offer that £74 was raised – including some money from someone role-playing a consultant – thereby covering the costs of the game.

The geographical layout of St Gabriel's Hall had an impact on the way the exercise turned out, so it is worth describing how the various groups involved in the game were spread about the building. The centre of things was the Chapel; here could be found the various BBC and commercial television groups, as well as the politicians and the Board of Broadcasting Control. The journalists, consultants and sponsorship fund administrators tended to hang out here as well. The members of the BBC's workforce were on their own in the Library, a room it took many of the participants some time to find, since it was down the corridor and round the corner from the Chapel. They had been put there with the intention that they would be cut off from the main action. The plan had been to hold a kind of "rolling tender" of programmes in here, but that is not what happened. This may have had something to do with the fact that the Library doors could be closed and undesirables excluded, something the workers turned to their advantage early on. Downstairs in the bar were Worldwide Distribution Inc. and the Independent Producers' Cartel, both with programmes to sell.

Year one

Not surprisingly, it took some time for the groups to settle down and work out that the money given (£2.55m in "cash", and another £1.2m in the form of a staff costs "voucher") had to cover all their services, not just network television – and that if they decided not to cut things they had to have the money for the other services in their hands at the end of year one.

From this point on, there were regular auctions of programmes, amidst other news announcements from the central desk. Programmes for sale included the Boat Race, a Tyson fight, and *The Three Tenors' Reunion Concert*, to raise money to help the Kurds. Many of these were acquired by ITV and BSkyB. News announcements included the establishment of a Broadcasting Sponsorship Fund, a commercial venture with £200,000 to spend on programme sponsorship. In the first session it had virtually no takers.

Towards the end of the session, the government announced it would review the performance of the groups in year one, and award different licence fees for year two, depending on the assessment of each group's performance in year one. Later still, there was news of an overnight election, the result of which was to be announced in the morning.

In terms of the outcome of the game, the most important thing was taking place in the BBC Production Centre. The workforce had predicted correctly that no matter what things were like in year one, they would get worse in year two, and its members therefore refused to talk to any of the groups until they were offered guarantees of future work. The intended rolling auction never happened. Instead, the pattern of events was as follows: a group would turn up with its voucher to spend £1.2m on programmes in year one, and the workforce would refuse to accept it until the group had committed to spend an equal amount in year two.

Astonishingly, all groups a contract to spend a minimum of £1.2m with the workforce in year two, and were apparently indifferent to the quality of the programmes they got in year one in exchange. Of five groups, only one attached any conditions, and even these were extremely vague.

Perhaps the power wielded by the workforce was a result of the combination of individuals; of the three participants playing the workforce, one was a BBC representative of the television trade union BECTU, and a second a training consultant versed in the mechanisms of simulation exercises. Perhaps it was a function of geography; they used their separate location as a lever, exploiting the fact that they were cut off from the rest off the game.

But one of the workers put their finger on a third factor. The workers had only one objective at the start of the game, which was to secure their continued income in year two, whereas the groups were being torn every which way by the demands of compiling a schedule, juggling budgets, and negotiating with other suppliers. The curious fact is that no group complained to the Board of Broadcasting Control about the workforce's negotiating tactics, yet they would have undoubtedly have benefited from doing so. Perhaps it was too early in the game for the haggling that developed later; maybe at that stage they had enough money to get by. Or maybe they just fell victim to Martin Amis's First Law of Street Fighting: Use The Maximum Amount Of Violence At The Earliest Possible Time.

At the end of year one, the groups' performances were as follows:

Group	Ratings	Prizes	Financial position
A	121 points	3	Deficit: £85,000 [1]
B	106 points	2	Surplus: £400,000
C	117 points	4	Surplus: £590,000
D	121 points	0	Deficit: 125,000 [2]
E	81 points	0	Deficit: £100,000 [3]

(1) Includes £1,050,000 "found" in apparently dodgy circumstances;

(2) The group's own accounts claimed a distinct surplus;

(3) Group E's financial position was adversely affected by its attempt to bribe the Minister, who eventually accepted £100,000 by way of a contribution to his favourite charity. But the attempt had no visible effect on their licence award.

Year two

At this stage, all groups' services remained intact, and all had signed a commitment to the workforce to spend £1.2m in year two. When the licence fee awards were made, all but one of the groups were in financial difficulties:

Group A, with concern about their financial management and too many entertainment programmes, received a licence fee of only £1.5m, along with £200,000 from Enterprises. But since the "dodgy" £1,050,000 was held back pending the result of an inquiry, at the start of the year they had commitments of £2.5m, but only £715,000 in the bank.

Group B's licence fee was set at £1.2m, a reflection of their poor ratings and the fact that they had carried a lot of hours forward. With £200,000 from Enterprises, and their year one profit, they had £2.5m in commitments, but only £1.8m in the bank.

Group C did well out of the review, with good ratings, good profits, award-winning programmes, and good accounts. (As the Minister, or perhaps one of his speechwriters, said, the Conservatives are pleased to reward excellence in all walks of life). A licence fee of £2m, £200,000 from Enterprises, profits of £590,000, their bank balance of £2,790,000 covered their fixed commitments of £2.5m. They were the only group ahead at this stage.

Group D's strong ratings were built on too much entertainment and no quality programmes, and although they were awarded a £1.5m licence fee, £500,000 was held back pending a consultant's report on their financial position. At the start of year one they had a bank balance of £1,075,000, but commitments of £2.5m.

Group E were bound to do badly in the licence review. Terrible ratings and no quality, together with a programming strategy which they claimed was directed at the European working-class, took their toll. A licence fee award of £1m, together with £200,000 from Enterprises, less a loss carried forward of £100,000, left them with assets of £1m – but commitments of £2.5m. Disaster was staring them in the face.

The result of the overnight election (a fix) had already been predicted in the Symposium newspaper, the *Manchester Daily Beast*:

"Election shock

"The Labour Party may be set for victory in today's election, which will result in the appointment of a new broadcasting minister.

"The man tipped for the post, Bevan Jones, told the Beast, 'We promise a new deal for broadcasting'.

"Asked if a new government would change the licence fee settlement imposed by the outgoing Tories, he said 'Frankly, we can't afford it.' " (*Manchester Daily Beast*, 11 April 1991)

The outgoing Conservative minister spent most of the £500,000 "Gulf levy" he had collected at the start of the game on a Trust for Broadcasting Excellence, which was dished out at the rate of £50,000 per prizewinning programme in year one. Group C collected another £200,000, Group A £150,000, and Group B £100,000.

So moved was the Labour Minister by this that he promptly announced that the Conservative ex-minister would investigate the mystery of Group A's "now you see it" cash. It was one of the fastest inquiries in history, possibly for electoral reasons; the published report read:

"I certify that I, formerly Her Majesty's Minister of State For Broadcasting, am satisfied with the financial probity of Group A and recommend full restoration of the funds due to them."

With a room almost full of BBC groups which were now trading illegally, it was only a matter of time before someone cracked: either other services, or the workforce contracts, were certain to give. Group D was the first to go: at 3pm on Thursday afternoon they announced that they were axing all radio services.

The financial squeeze was quickly felt as new projects came up for auction – the BBC groups were bidding lower, and were usually outbid by the commercial companies, now operating an informal and certainly illegal cartel. No one protested. BSkyB bought League Football and Channel 3 the Grand National, the Beatles Reunion Concert and Kiri Te Kanawa's Last Farewell Concert.

Before then, the commercial stations had already done an output deal with the Independent Producers' Cartel, securing all their entertainment programming for the commercial sector, which pushed the BBC groups more towards factual programming; few could afford much in the way of drama. By this stage, in negotiations with the workforce, the groups were mostly told that they would get whatever was available when the money was forthcoming.

But curiously, few opted for the lure of sponsored programming, even though there was £2m there waiting to be spent, which could have gone to any one group prepared to do the right deal. Perhaps the Sponsorship Fund's ever lengthening list of increasingly tasteless clients was a deterrent. The inside story of the Fund had been carried by the *Manchester Daily Beast*, that morning:

"Sponsorship body takeover bid

"The replacement of John Gray as chief executive of the Broadcast Sponsorship Fund is likely to be announced this morning.

"The new chief executive is likely to be Jerome Cuelo, who has resigned as managing director of the New Jersey and Palermo-based Media International to take up his new post. BSF funding will be increased to £2m.

"Mr Cuelo is expected to bring new clients to the BSF, including the International Atomic Energy Association, the Anglo-Am Tobacco Corporation of South Africa, the International Armaments Council, and the International Field Sports League." (*Manchester Daily Beast*, 11 April 1991)

By now it was nearly teatime, and there were rumours of another election in the offing. Some notes from that period:

■ Members of Group E take the Labour Broadcasting Minister aside and offer a deal. They are so short of money that they are going to have to scrap all their radio channels, including their community radio services, unless the government can help out. They know how committed he is to community radio, and of course would love to develop their radio services in that direction, if only he could find the odd million pounds. Some horsetrading later, and a loan is agreed – £1m, repayable by the end of the second session. Group E breathes again.

■ Rumours abound that the Liberal Democrat spokesperson has been kidnapped. Certainly she is nowhere to be found, and there are frantic efforts by the Liberal Democrat fixer to postpone the election until she can be located.

■ Kidnap fever strikes, because there are news reports that the Queen has been kidnapped in Yugoslavia. Special news coverage packages are offered by the control desk, in the form of jokers – but no group has enough money to buy one.

■ One group tries to get a bank off the ground. They talk to the executives of the Sponsorship Fund, who say they already own all the banks they need. The distributors and the independent producers, both of whom have money, are reported not to be interested.

■ One group threatens to sue the Board of Broadcasting Control for alleged impropriety. It settles out of court, £100,000 richer.

■ The Government announces a licence fee rebate for all pensioners – cost, 10% of licence fee award. But shortly afterwards a new scheme is announced, to encourage public service broadcasting. Factual programmes will be subsidized to the value of £10,000 per ratings point, and news £10,000 per programme. But before the scheme can be implemented, an election is called, and the Conservative shadow Minister promises to scrap both ideas if he is returned.

A consultant appointed to review the activities of Group D reported: "The Finance Director was dismissed at the end of last year. A new Finance Director (wearing suit) has been appointed. I suggest you restore all lines of credit to the group."

At this point, another election took place. This second election was the most important single event in the game, for the politician who won would choose the winner of the game after the second session. It was not a fix. Instead, the players voted, and the Conservative won. Votes cast were: Conservative 19, Labour 18, the Liberal Democrats 16, Frank Sinatra Appreciation 1, Greens 1.

As promised, the Conservative promptly ended Labour's plans to cut the licence fee to help pensioners, to the apparent relief of the groups, a bit tight for cash at the time. But calls for a recount revealed the election to be a tie: 18 votes apiece. This was not a fix either, though it may have involved some cheating.

Consequently, there had to be a new election. Before it was called, a blind member of Group E negotiated with the Conservative Broadcasting Minister a £1m government grant for a "disability project". The Minister viewed the scheme as "very impressive", and said that he was pleased to be able to help. The project was later discovered to have cost a fraction of this. If any of the other groups knew of this none complained.

The second poll result revealed a massive landslide to both Labour and the Frank Sinatra Appreciation Party (which doubled its vote to 2). Conservative 11, Lib. Dem. 16, Labour 32.

The reason for the landslide was never clear, although it did not appear to be ballot rigging (except for the Frank Sinatra votes). It may be that in the meantime groups had calculated that the Public Service Rebate was going to bring in more revenue than the amount they would lose from the cut in their licence fee.[1]

The groups now had about 20 minutes to ensure that their programming plans would meet with the approval of a Labour Government. But the biggest surprise was still to come. Group E issued the following press statement:

> "Group E undertakes to introduce workers' representatives onto the board of the company. At least 51% of the board are to be workers. Further, at least 53% of the board are to be women. In consequence Group E reaffirms its belief in the radio service and guarantees that the funding of the radio service will continue at its present level.

> "(Signed) David Hallan for Group E.

> "Full co-operation of the workforce is guaranteed.

> "(Signed) Luke Crawley for the workforce."

Despite Group E's various political initiatives, it was still short of money. Members of the group approached the workforce and explained that they could not afford both to meet their contract from year one and to keep radio services running. The workforce proposed that its members would work for nothing on radio – the alternative was being unemployed – but that in exchange the workers would effect what amounted to a reverse takeover of Group E, which included bringing the various sums they had accumulated in their deals with *all* the groups in year two. (Again, no-one else complained).

Most of the members of Group E promptly resigned – the former Director-General took a large pay-off and announced that he was setting himself up in the Isle of Man as a tax-efficient independent. (The workforce – all male – had to insist that a woman member stayed on to act as Director-General, which had been one of their conditions in making the takeover).

---

1 According to Jim Brown, the workforce bribed members of the electorate at this point (see his account, p. 111) – Eds.

The Isle of Man independent was able to strike a good deal, too. When the rights to Mrs Thatcher's funeral became available, late on in the game, he was able to pick them up cheap (he was at this stage virtually the only player in the game with spare money) and re-sell them at a profit to a group which had discovered it needed another independent production to reach its quota.

The outcome

The final presentations took place in the Granada House of Commons set, after the "Parliamentary" debate had finished – which must be the second worst place in the country to give them, after the real House of Commons. There is something about the place which encourages long speeches where short ones will do, and discourages people from listening. Furthermore, the available time had been squeezed by an over-run of the debate.

Group A had cut no services, and it had liquid assets of £1,355,000 (including £380,000 in Public Service Rebate) to cover the £1.3m needed to run its radio and regional TV. This group was one of the few to take a programme ("Fur Is Fun") from the Sponsorship Fund, and ran it in prime time – but followed it with a discussion about the pros and cons of such programmes. "The phone-in, and the letters we received, show that the public do not want BBC programmes to be financed in this way", said a spokesperson for the group. Group A also claimed to be showing "The Nancy Tapes" – the film of the Kitty Kelley biography.

Group B was also showing "The Nancy Tapes", which led to accusations of piracy. It had merged Radios 1 and 2, and also Radios 3 and 4, and was running a "bi-media" regional TV service, which it claimed was innovative but was also cheap (£780,000 the lot). To pay for these additional services, it had liquid assets of £670,000 (£480,000 in Public Service Rebate). The shortfall was to come from a sponsorship deal which was still being fixed up (and was never finalized). Since the Labour Minister was a great fan of radio, cutting services put this group out of the frame immediately. Group B was lucky not to be disqualified for being bankrupt.

Group C was in some disarray. It had cut nothing, but it only had £585,000 in the bank (£315,000 in cash, and £270,000 in Public Service Rebate). It claimed that its women's rugby programme was being sponsored by the government, although the government was vague on this. It gained some bonus points for its programme "Jingo" – a game show based on Peter Snow's *Newsnight* sandpit. Group C had also done a deal with Channel 4 for one showing of a drama to which Channel 4 owned the rights – one of the few examples of commercial sector co-operating with BBC. Again, it was lucky not to be disqualified for being bankrupt.

Group D's response to the activities of the Broadcast Sponsorship Fund was an *Inside Story* documentary investigating the Fund's Palermo connections. Otherwise, its emphasis was claimed to be on fun, and although references were made to studio drama and innovative arts programming, the schedule the group produced featured three hours of drama, six hours of entertainment, and three hours of sport. One planned programme, made possible by the change of government, was "Douglas Hurd's Big Night Out". Although Group D was in the black, it had achieved this position by cutting all radio services, and all regional TV, which again ruled it out of contention as far as the government was concerned.

Group E was now a fully fledged worker's co-op and had renamed itself the British Workers' Broadcasting Corporation. It had money and services coming out of its ears. It promised David Hare films and a classic drama serial based loosely on the Chartist movement. But it also had Little and Large, and Les Dawson, and *Give 'Em A Break*.

Of course, it won. As the worker-directors drank their bottle of champagne over lunch they argued about whether they were turning into statist bureaucrats or whether, now the workers were in charge, all BBC employees would drink champagne.

Observations

1. It was a complex game. The need to control budgets, while also monitoring frequent announcements (some essential, most not), and dealing with several sources of programming, meant that groups were stretched, especially since some members of each team started drifting away by Thursday lunchtime. I was impressed by how quickly the members – not all of whom were broadcasting professionals – got to grips with the complexities of the task they were being asked to perform.

2. The commercial channels had less impact than expected. They used their superior buying power (especially once the cartel emerged) to clean up the big events. But there were surprisingly few deals done: they largely kept to themselves, even though they were based in the same area as the BBC groups. Perhaps because they had a less central stake in the game, they had a different approach to it.

3. The journalists and consultants built into the game also had less impact than expected (although they did stir things up helpfully from time to time). This may have been because we decided early on that anyone who wished to make a statement could have access to the microphone in the Chapel, rather than have to make a statement through the media.

4. The one group which had a greater impact than expected was the politicians. The various BBC groups realized very early that pleasing the politicians was the key to eventual success, and there were continual discussions going on in huddles in various parts of the Chapel between the politicians and the broadcasters. As members of one group told me afterwards, they had been busy for most of the game, except for a 20-minute lull in the middle of Thursday afternoon while waiting for the final election result. It was quite like life, in fact.

5. A final note, on sealed bids: the prices offered in the envelopes for the Beatles reunion concert with Julian Lennon ranged from £60,000 to £400,000; for three hours of cricket from £30,000 to £215,000. Neither of these is a Channel 3 franchise. But I think the ITC might be surprised by the divergence in the price people working from the same information are prepared to pay for the same thing.

Conclusion

One of the great pleasures of designing simulation exercises is that things never quite turn out how you expect them to, and "It's Your BBC" was no exception. When we were writing it, we discussed a number of likely outcomes as the financial squeeze began to bite in year two – and I do not think that I am giving away any secrets when I say that none of them involved the workers mounting a reverse takeover of one of the groups.

The other pleasure of a simulation exercise lies in the way in which its "virtual reality" offers insights into the workings of the real world. I think that the outcome of "It's Your BBC" is a case in point.

By this I do not mean that the salvation of the BBC lies in handing over its management to committees of workers, technicians and producers, enlivening though such a development might be. Instead, the clues are in the manner in which the workers achieved their *coup de grâce*.

One of the reasons for the triumph of the workers lay simply in a quirk in the construction of the game; they were sitting on a pile of money which in the real world would long since have gone on paying the mortgage. But that was also true of other groups – such as the independent producers and international distributors – who had also accumulated piles of money by the end of the game.

The second reason the workers won was because they had a clear broadcasting strategy, and they actively looked for the opportunity to implement. Eventually they found a group which was in a weak enough position to be willing to negotiate with them. They might have won even without the money.

This second reason is reflected in the way that the groups responded when they found themselves short of money at the beginning of year two. At that point, only one group, Group C, had more cash than commitments. Judging from its distinguished performance in year one, I had tipped this group privately as the almost certain winner. In fact, this group fell apart. When I asked the group members about this afterwards, they said they thought it was precisely because they had had enough money – or at least enough to get by – that they blew it. Because they had enough money, they did not have to make the tough decisions about what they had to do; instead they let things drift while others were getting on with it.

Group E, on the other hand, which ended up being taken over by the workforce, had been in desperate straits at the end of year one. Members of this group said that it was precisely because they were in such deep trouble that they had to take hard decisions about how to stay afloat. What set Group E apart from other groups whose financial plight was almost as severe (and who responded quite rationally by cutting services) was that its response was initially a political one. I do not know how they did it, but the members of this group persuaded government ministers to find more money to put into broadcasting, by fastening onto the ministers' pet projects.

It was not clear from where I was sitting whether this group ended up making the deal which won it the game by being the right group, with the right problem, in the right place, at the right time, or whether it won by being open to ideas, and by being politically astute. The merger or takeover was formally announced only as the result of the final election became known: had the Conservative won, he was unlikely to have chosen Group E as the winner.

Nonetheless, I think there is a lesson here for the real world. It seems to me that, as the licence fee continues to fall in real terms, the BBC management is more likely to find itself in the position of Group C, which has just about enough to get by for the time being, rather than that of one which is staring bankruptcy in the face.

If I am right, the BBC may never be under fierce enough pressure to think it worth building the public and political campaign which is essential to protect the idea of public service broadcasting in the face of multi-channel competition. It will never be hard enough up against the wall to have to ask the difficult questions about what it is that is distinctive about the BBC, what it is that we need most to cherish and protect, and what it is that should be fought for when the going gets really tough.

"It's Your BBC – Now Run It" was devised by Andrew Curry, with assistance from Jerry Kuehl, Steve Barnett and Robin McCron.

10 How the British Workers' Broadcasting Corporation won the day: A participant's view of the symposium

Jim Brown
Independent consultant and management trainer

Perhaps the sternest test to which any conference can be subjected is whether or not it is intelligible to someone not connected with the subject under scrutiny. For the last three years I have been invited to the Manchester Broadcasting Symposium, not because of any involvement I have in broadcasting, but to provide an evaluation of the event. My qualifications for this task are that I am a consultant working in the field of organizational behaviour, and hence I might best be described as a professional participant.

I do have one other qualification. Over the last eight years Symposium Director Nod Miller and I have worked together on the design and development of participative events. Our mission has been to make such events more effective vehicles for learning, networking and enjoyment. This is in contrast to conventional conference designs, which mainly feature long, boring platform speeches counteracted only by the chummy cliques in the bar afterwards. Such designs are only tolerated, I suspect, because conference goers have such low expectations of conferences.

The main mechanisms adopted in the Manchester Symposium for achieving more effective participation are the participative group exercise and the House of Commons debate, both of which are described in some detail elsewhere in this book. Other mechanisms include the emphasis on panel discussions, which bring together people of differing views and encourage contributions, questions and challenges from the audience. This year even the evening entertainment was participative, involving a game show designed by Action Time.

Day one

As a lapsed Catholic it came as a shock when I realized that my three days at the

Symposium would be spent sitting in a chapel. Surrounded by the Stations of the Cross and a 12 foot Crucifix, I struggled with my conscience and impure thoughts. Should I try harder this year to keep my big mouth shut ? Did I recognize that rather attractive person from last year ? Fantasies filled my head. I tried to look nonchalant; after all TV executives are no longer as powerful, rich and sexy as they used to be.

The opening panel session set out the consensus view that the BBC was of major cultural importance and, rather like Stonehenge, must be preserved as part of our national heritage. The threat came from grey suits. These grey suits were intent upon robbing the Great British Public of their constitutional rights to part gleefully with large sums of money in the form of a licence fee, which was being used to fund other grey suits wickedly engaged in preventing those without grey suits from making extremely worthy programmes of a public service nature. Clearly grey suits were the enemy.

With an urgent sense of public duty ringing in our ears we set off for Whitworth Hall to hear from Anthony Smith, the keynote speaker. The use of a keynote speaker is the single concession to conventional conference design, and it had been decided, appropriately, that the grander surroundings of Whitworth Hall were called for. Buses had been laid on for the one mile journey, but eager and impatient, I decided I needed the exercise and started off on foot. Unfortunately, I assumed the people in front of me knew where they were going. After a detour, which took in the Whitworth Art Gallery and most of the University campus, I arrived at Whitworth Hall for the end of tea and biscuits, but in time for Anthony Smith.

This man has been everything in his time – a board member of Channel 4, director of the BFI, a member of the Arts Council, producer of *24 Hours*, Annan committee member and now President of Magdalen College, Oxford: a veritable public service mandarin. He talked about the future of the BBC and public service broadcasting. "If only they had listened to the Annan committee," he cried. The problem, once again, turned out to be grey suits.

Breaking a holy abstinence of at least two hours, I asked him how he would democratize the BBC and make it more accountable to the public it serves. He wrung his hands, shook his head and expressed his doubts. "We have tried our hardest, but there is no easy solution to this question of democracy." He wasn't being evasive – at least I did not think he was.

Back at St Gabriel's I cornered Anthony Smith in the bar. I confessed my overwhelming sense of sycophancy in the presence of Establishment figures such as himself. He looked shocked. "There really is no Establishment; anybody determined enough can work their way into the corridors of power." I asked him how he became a member of the Arts Council; was he elected by the public ? "Well," he said, "it's a very small world, you know. After a while you realize that everybody knows everybody else".

After dinner it was round one of the group exercise "It's Your BBC – Now Run It". Andrew Curry had taken the precaution of confining me to a side role, representing the BBC workforce, with whom the groups playing the exercise would negotiate for programmes. I was teamed up with Luke Crawley, who is on the national executive of BECTU, and Calum Gillies, an M.Ed student from Manchester University.

109

We were responsible for negotiating which programmes we would "sell" to the five groups competing to "run" the BBC. In this first round we were guaranteed sales, but in the next round the groups were not obliged to "buy" from us. It took us five minutes to devise our strategy. We would offer groups absolutely anything they wanted in the first round, so long as they would give us a written guarantee promising us security for the second round. We embellished our story about how our only concern was preserving jobs for the future.

One by one the BBC groups signed the deals guaranteeing our future. In return they had their pick of our programmes at bargain prices. It did not seem to occur to groups that they were all being offered the same deal. Even the final group, to whom we were only able to offer the paltry remains of a once-rich programme list, seemed convinced that they had struck the deal of the century.

Day two

The day began with a panel discussion about the future possibilities of advertising on the BBC. Harold Lind, consultant, made himself unpopular by arguing that there was no alternative but to accept advertising. Libby Child, advertiser, made herself even more unpopular by snapping up the offer. "Surveys show that people like TV adverts" she claimed. Gillian Laidlaw, management consultant, said it was all to do with organizational culture. Apparently culture is something management consultants are very good at. Finally, Richard Wade, Director-General of the Advertising Association, addressed the audience, which was by now anticipating the worst. "What I am about to say does not represent the views of the Advertising Association" he confided. "Nor shall I express my own views," he added somewhat confusingly. Clearly he was not in a mood to give anything away.

The audience by now was ready to rid the gathering of those who might pollute the BBC with advertisements. "What's so wrong with the licence fee?" several voices demanded. Research had shown that the Great British Public were happy to fork out at least 20% more money on licences. Never mind the fact that that licence fee dodgers outnumber poll tax evaders two to one.

The next session offered a choice between a panel on the future of BBC Radio and another panel on engineering issues and the introduction of high definition television. I plumped for the latter. I'm afraid I cannot recall much about this session, having got slightly confused about the difference between PAL and dog food, but I do remember coming away with the lasting impression that the Japanese were up to no good. Japanese television manufacturers, having made the fatal mistake of designing televisions that never break down, are apparently trying to convince broadcasters to transmit programmes that require everyone to buy a new TV.

The afternoon was devoted to round two of the group exercise. Luke, Calum and I had a five minute strategy meeting and decided that now we had cast-iron job guarantees from every BBC group, we would devote ourselves to high quality public service broadcasting. It would also be highly expensive, or, as we preferred to describe it, very time-consuming. We could only produce half the number of programmes for the same amount of money as in round one. The groups protested, but caved in when we showed them their written guarantees. One group did manage to blackmail us into providing the full quota of hours, reminding us that we had suggested that the guarantee they signed was an exclusive one-off deal.

Group E was a different story. They did not have the money to honour the guarantee, having spent it all on preserving local radio. Like a flash, we offered them a historic deal. Give us, the workforce, majority control of the Board of Governors, and you can have what you want for whatever you can afford. After a little negotiation over gender quotas on the Board the deal was struck and the British Workers' Broadcasting Corporation was born. Our only task now was to ensure the return of a Labour Government. Using the cash mountain acquired from our earlier sales of pro-grammes, we bribed the electorate into providing a comfortable majority for Labour.

With the game stitched up in our favour I made my way to the third panel discussion of the day, devoted to the broadcast coverage of the Gulf War. ITN's Glyn Mathias and the BBC's Clive Ferguson gave almost identical performances, a mixture of reasoned and weary seriousness. Dissenting voices were provided by Tory MP Geoffrey Dickens and media academic John Eldridge. Dickens waded in over the coverage of the bunker/shelter bombing, evidence as he saw it of the BBC and ITN being conned by Iraqi propaganda. The Great British Public did not need to know about this, Dickens declared, to barely bated gasps from the audience.

Eldridge, a self proclaimed critic of the concept of objectivity, showed us his top ten favourite snippets of Gulf War coverage, followed by an Islington bar room analysis of what we had seen. He seemed oblivious of the fact that media analysis is just about the most popular parlour room game in existence and that most of the audience had already endured months of such armchair commentary back at home.

Dickens knew he was obliged to have a go at Eldridge so he weighed in with the startling accusation that Eldridge was biased, thereby demonstrating his complete ignorance of the practised art of critical subjectivity. Meanwhile, Mathias and Fergu-son continued to be seriously reasonable and weary. No one proffered the popular analysis current in my pub that the Americans had targeted the bunker because it was packed with the wives and children of senior ranking Iraqi officers.

Later that evening there was panel discussion number four of the day. I did not attend. I have no excuse. Afterwards, I asked one or two people what the session was like. They seemed confused. One panel too many I fear.

To round the evening off Action Time, game show producers *extraordinaire*, extracted their revenge on all those broadcasters who refuse to categorize game shows as a public service, by subjecting us to the oral equivalent of Manchester University's M.Ed in Media Studies final examinations.

Day three

This was day of the great debate in Granada Studios' House of Commons set. Under debate was the Broadcasting Bill of 1996. Proposed by Barbara Hosking, political consultant to YTV and opposed by Jocelyn Hay, of the Voice of the Listener, the Bill that promised to savage the BBC was itself savaged by both sides of the House.

111

Barbara Hosking had devised a unique method of nobbling the opposition, which consisted of immediately accepting every amendment they could muster.

When she hastily accepted an amendment which demanded that every Governor on the BBC Board should be directly elected by the public we knew the game was up. Having won every amendment, the opposition was so confused that they threw out the Bill on the final vote. At a stroke, the gains of the day were cast into the dustbin of nice but silly ideas. No doubt many at the BBC would be perfectly happy if such fantasy were to turn to reality in five years' time.

And so to the end of the Symposium. The winners of the group exercise were announced. No surprises there when we knew the judge was the Labour Minister for Broadcasting from the day before. Our team, the British Workers' Broadcasting Corporation gratefully collected the bottle of champagne, which supplemented the already generous Granada lunch time booze-up.

Postscript

If I were the symposium organizers I would ban me from taking part in the group exercise. It is far too easy for anyone with a modicum of understanding of group processes to win. I made this point two years ago when the group I was in also won the group exercise.

As for the House of Commons debate, there still seems to be a missing ingredient. This year there was no opposition, or to be more accurate, no opposition to the opposition. This reflects perhaps the homogeneity of view amongst the participants attracted to the Symposium, which is not surprising given that the Symposium bills itself as "the premier forum for the debate of public service broadcasting policy".

The problem is that there is no real debate. Everyone present supports the concept of public service broadcasting, an easy consensus that overwhelms the sensibilities for three days, allowing us to create a paradise where men and women are equal, workers are represented on the Board of Management and governors are elected by a public who are happy to pay ever larger licence fees: a paradise where news journalists are factual, accurate and objective and media academics are critical, analytical and sceptical. Above all it is a paradise where the output of BBC TV and Radio is a perfect example of public service broadcasting.

I am not knocking a bit of solidarity; goodness only knows that this is necessary in the current climate. But where is the social change ? The BBC, in my eyes at least, remains the most visible pillar of the British Establishment. Fed on a constantly rich diet of Oxbridge graduates, the BBC remains firmly on its feet with its paws rammed inside the honeypot provided by the licence payer.

I could sense an air of dissatisfaction with the BBC, but everyone was frightened that to wave goodbye to the BBC would mean the end of public service broadcasting. Confronted with the opportunity for social change, we, being British, prefer social order.

A decade of Thatcherism has dulled our resistance to the prospect of consensus politics that threatens to overwhelm the nineties. Back in the Wilson-Heath era, I almost lost faith in parliamentary politics, there being so little difference between the two parties. That era seems to be re-emerging with Major and Kinnock. Under consensus politics the Establishment are given a free hand to look after their own sort. Never mind if public service programmes are not popular with the public, so long as they are popular with the minority who believe in public service broadcasting.

Throughout the Symposium I wondered, but dared not ask, what constituted public service broadcasting. The impression I got is that any programme "we" like could be counted as public service broadcasting. This presumably excludes game shows, sitcoms and foreign soaps. Drama may be a public service so long as it is heavyweight. The same applies to documentaries. Current affairs including religion is public service. Education definitely is, except when it is about cooking. Music definitely is not, unless it is Art or ethnic. All local programmes are public service, whatever their quality.

Serving the public through broadcasting raises thorny old Gramscian problems about the relationship between the State and civil society (Gramsci's term for the public). The BBC is bound to the State by the purse strings. To maintain appearances the State distances itself from direct control, relying instead on the Establishment to secure the status quo on its behalf. This cosy relationship goes unchallenged under consensus politics. Introduce a radical, like Thatcher, and the careful balance is disturbed. She believed in capitalism, not consensus. The Establishment was under threat.

Unfortunately for Thatcher, capitalism failed to deliver, and the Establishment is experiencing a brief reprieve. The short term economic gains for the few have all but evaporated under the relentless pressure of long term economic decline in Britain. We used to make high quality programmes, but the truth is, as with so many other things such as the education system and the health service, we can no longer afford it as a nation. Taxing the public, albeit through the indirect mechanism of the licence fee, has reached the point of no return. Unless we can earn more as a nation, we will have to learn to cope with less.

I cannot escape the conclusion that the argument for public service broadcasting, as a concept, is nothing more than a plea for a by-gone age, a Great Britain with a beneficent Establishment maintaining social order. Those days have gone.

Public service broadcasting must commit itself to social change. This means risking to the limit the relationship that exists between the broadcaster and the state. It is a challenge confronting the broadcasting Establishment, not only of the BBC, but also of the independent companies. Furthermore, it is a challenge to all those who work in the broadcast medium to recast the mould of public service as something concerned with social change, not social order. Perhaps we unwittingly threw away the solution with the amended Broadcasting Bill of 1996. Or perhaps the solution lay with the British Workers' Broadcasting Corporation. Only time will tell.

11 Safe in whose hands? The BBC and the nineties

Steven Barnett

Head of Media Futures, Henley Centre for Economic Forecasting

At least with the National Health Service, Mrs Thatcher's rhetoric was unambiguous. We may have heard the unmistakable rattle of dismantling in the background, but the constant refrain from Downing Street was "safe in our hands".

No such certainty ever afflicted Prime Ministerial statements on that other very British (though not quite so universally admired) institution, the BBC. In 11 years of office, Thatcher government expressions of support, affection or even tolerance of the Corporation were as frequent as hand-outs for the homeless. But John Major, according to first impressions, is different. If precedent is anything to go by, his apparent support, or at least lack of blatant hostility, will survive at least until the first day of the General Election campaign. If not John Major, then certainly the Freedom Association or some other surrogate body will be raising the spectre of bias and the need for control before too long.

Lest we delude ourselves that such intimidation is the sole preserve of an unforgiving Conservative Party, we should cast our minds back beyond the dozen uninterrupted years of Tory government to the last two Labour prime ministers. Harold Wilson's legendary paranoia about the BBC's subversive intent led him to endorse what was then a radical plan (originated by Tony Benn) designed to reduce its power: force it to take advertising and hive off radio (in the days before "privatization" became a fashionable word). The plan was dropped only after intense BBC lobbying, causing Richard Crossman to complain to the Board of Management about an "all-powerful Corporation" capable of overturning a British Cabinet decision.[1]

Ten years later, the affable and avuncular Callaghan was equally rattled by what he saw as a BBC conspiracy against Trade Unions and the Left. His solution for restoring balance was a proposal to introduce a new level of management, appointed by the Home Office and therefore introducing direct Government interference for the first time. The plans were published in a White Paper, the BBC again mounted an effective

---

1 Recorded in *Live From Number 10* by Michael Cockerell, Faber & Faber, 1988.

resistance (with the help of almost unanimous press opposition to the proposals), and the plans were again dumped.

So we should not be complacent about this comparative calm after the several storms of the last decade. Yes, we seem to be facing a period of (relative) political consensus with voting choices limited to the respectable right or reformed left. And, yes, there is a temporary respite in vilification campaigns aimed at the BBC. There is even a document published by the Tory Reform Group – unthinkable just a year ago – which explicitly states "The Conservative Party should make it clear that the BBC is safe in our hands"[1]. But there are two very good reasons why the BBC will not be left for long in such relative tranquillity.

The first is a tabloid press whose hysteria knows no bounds in its furious denunciation of the Corporation's actual or invented errors. In stark contrast to Fleet Street's response 15 years ago to Callaghan's clumsy attempts at direct control, any similar proposal today would be eagerly seized upon by the tabloids. It is not just the News International newspapers pursuing a proprietorial interest in rubbishing a crucial obstacle to Sky's success. The *Daily Express* revels in fallacious stories of "BBC bias" (and even paid the Media Monitoring Unit for its transparently political and spurious "study"), and the *Daily Mail* is rarely sympathetic. There are few friends among the Press.[2]

The second reason is the charter and licence renewal due in 1996 and the excuse this offers political parties for meddling. Combined with the so-called (and much exaggerated) "revolution" provided by satellite channels, here is a heaven-sent opportunity to recast the broadcasting ecology in a mould more suited to a particular ideology. In other words, any change to the BBC can be camouflaged beneath the "inevitable consequence" of a multi-channel future which renders the notion of a compulsory licence fee redundant. Warning shots have already been fired in the first think-tank forays into deliberating the BBC's future. In their different ways, both sides of the ideological spectrum have emerged with radical ideas for transforming the BBC. And in their different ways, the emerging policy papers are every bit as sinister and threatening to the fabric of public service broadcasting as the most pernicious Thatcherite rhetoric about free markets.

Given the uncompromising nature of most output from the Centre for Policy Studies, their document *A Better BBC* starts promisingly.[3] It accepts at the very beginning that "value judgements are to be made about individual programmes, or about television channels, beyond those made by audience ratings and market forces". It even talks about the importance of culture, or rather "culture". This is, reassuringly, Home Office speak, rather than the Trade and Industry speak which characterized much of the original White Paper on Broadcasting. It proceeds with the familiar argument that the broadcasting landscape will be transformed by satellite and cable and that therefore the BBC's share will fall dramatically. And then the crunch: "Those who

---

1 *What Shall We Do About the BBC?* by Stephen Milligan, Tory Reform Group, March 1991.
2 Any lingering doubts about the importance of proprietorial influence should be rapidly quashed by reading *Stick It Up Your Punter: the rise and fall of The Sun*, by Peter Chippindale and Chris Horrie, Heinemann, 1990.
3 *A Better BBC*, by Damian Green, Centre For Policy Studies, 1991.

believe that the existing system provides benefits which are worth conserving should recognize that the status quo of a compulsory licence fee with all proceeds paid to the BBC is bound to become indefensible". And further on: "If the BBC's audience share is inevitably set to plunge for reasons outside the Corporation's control, then radical alterations to the licence fee system are also inevitable".

This is the CPS rationale for its proposed Public Service Broadcasting Authority which, as Anthony Smith suggests, would distribute the licence revenue to bidders of whom the BBC would be just one suitor amongst many. Disingenuously, or very naïvely, this government-appointed body is described as "an important non-governmental check on the Corporation's efficiency and performance".

While the reformed right are prepared to tolerate the licence fee as long as it is distributed to all comers by government-appointed luminaries, the respectable left are proposing to abolish it altogether. The rationale quoted by the Institute for Public Policy Research is identical: "The licence fee belongs to the first age of monopoly. Its rationale became shaky in the second age of duopoly. With an estimated 8 million satellite dishes on British walls by the mid-1990s, its life has surely come to an end".[1] It is a new and untested logic that casts doubt on the efficacy of licence fee funding after ITV's emergence in 1955. That aside, what of the IPPR's conclusions? The answer is in a repudiation of the arms-length principle which has traditionally underpinned the licence fee: "The theory that the licence fee confers some special immunity from the demands of a rapacious Treasury has proved false". And therefore "the cost of the public services provided by the BBC [should] become a direct charge upon the taxpayer".

It is certainly true that there is an uncomfortable dependence on government disposition to accept licence fee rises, and that this is discreetly – sometimes blatantly – exploited by governments of all political hue. But to suggest that a battle between BBC and Home Secretary is a more corrosive process than that between Treasury and an indirectly represented supplicant organization underestimates Treasury power in setting spending limits. An increase in the licence fee represents a tiny increase in the Retail Price Increase, the only political sacrifice involved for an incumbent government. An equivalent increase via direct subvention cannot possibly be easier to negotiate around a Cabinet table full of frustrated colleagues who are sacrificing hospital beds, school books, and road or transport improvements.

It is always easier to criticize than to propose. But when a system is as finely balanced as British broadcasting, the changes being proposed by these political think-tanks risk the risk of causing irreparable damage for no apparent return. When the Peacock Committee was in the midst of its deliberations, it was widely repeated that "the status quo is not an option" for the BBC. It may be that, in terms of funding and its relationship with the state, the status quo is the only option.

This is particularly true at a time when the private sector is undergoing such fundamental upheaval. Once the new applicants are in place, the process of recouping massive auction bids will start and pressure will grow to ditch lower rating pro-

1 *The Third Age of Broadcasting,* by David Boulton, Institute for Public Policy Research, forthcoming.

grammes. From 1994, ITV companies will be looking over their shoulders for likely takeover bids, a further impetus for cost-cutting and audience-boosting. That is the television environment in which the BBC will be competing. It needs to be in stable, vigorous shape to stand by its own priorities and continue setting the standards for other broadcasters to follow. More importantly, it must be competent to fulfil those roles which are most at risk when the competitive heat rises: training, schools and education programmes, arts and music programmes, expensive outside broadcasts which are part of the country's heritage, children's programmes and radio drama. The BBC as a truly independent cultural force needs a licence fee. The key to constructive change in its relationship with the state is not to concede that political patronage is inevitable and therefore embrace it totally; it is to search for mechanisms, structures, or statutory obligations which help to minimize the risk of political interference under any but the most ruthlessly authoritarian administration (at which point we can all give up and go home anyway).

A frisson of the pressure that will afflict the BBC as the independent sector becomes truly competitive was conveyed during the simulation exercise at this year's Symposium. In between second guessing election results and the policy vagaries of respective broadcasting ministers, BBC teams were faced with funding their own public service visions from a declining revenue base against overtly populist commercial channels. We began to appreciate how vulnerable the less high profile BBC activities were to emergency cost-cutting exercises: in particular, local radio and Radios 1 and 2 became hard to justify when coping with massive retrenchment.

There is an unfortunate but growing tendency, even amongst BBC supporters, to consign Radio 1 and Radio 2 to privatized oblivion without any real analysis or appreciation of their contribution. Perhaps we should not be surprised, since the Peacock Committee allegedly spent all of half a day on its radio deliberations before coming to precisely those conclusions. Even those who are prepared to concede the importance of mass audience programming on BBC television find themselves incapable of applying the same logic to radio. But take away those two stations, and where is the relevance of BBC radio to the vast majority of people? Those who would deprive the nation of Radio 1 – and they will become more numerous and more vociferous as commercial radio goes national – should perhaps be reminded that over 90% of under 35s have at some stage been Radio 1 listeners.

Radio 2 has a less defined audience and will suffer most as the new breed of AM "golden oldie" stations proliferate. But both stations, and local radio too, will maintain the one difference which will infuriate their critics and endear them at least to some listeners – lack of advertising. If freedom of choice is one of the key criteria of our new broadcasting system, then is not the freedom to choose a station without commercial messages an integral part of that process?

This is equally applicable to television and becomes increasingly important as advertising minuteage increases, as sponsorship rules are relaxed and as new commercially funded radio and TV stations are added to the existing repertoire. Even with its promotions for *Radio Times*, BBC videos and other Enterprise offers, the BBC will still represent a haven for those seeking some respite from the increasing commoditization of broadcasting.

This process does not only apply to on-screen messages but to the very nature of programming. Commercial revenue is vital to the enhancement of a thriving and vibrant broadcasting industry. In the past, that revenue has been harnessed by programme makers and not become their master. As competition for this revenue intensifies, commercial channels and stations will be increasingly pressurized into making creative concessions to keep their patrons happy; at that point, a healthy non-commercial sector free of such influences becomes more vital than ever. It is ironic that the BBC's survival as a powerful non-commercial alternative might depend on its not taking too large a slice out of the commercial audience. If the BBC defies all expectations and actually maintains a 50% share of total viewing and listening, neither political party may prove strong enough to withstand the strictures of the advertising industry.

What the Symposium exercise could not embrace, but what emerged most forcefully in the "Parliamentary debate" of the following day, was the pervasive problem of accountability and seeming inaccessibility of the BBC. While it spends an enormous amount of money on audience research to keep in touch with its various listening and viewing constituencies, the vast majority of its findings remains confidential and thus unacknowledged. This has two consequences: it serves to reinforce the image of an unresponsive organization which fails to consult the wishes and needs of those it serves; and it hampers the development of a proper dialogue between service provider and service users. There is a precarious balance between maintaining confidential information that is vital to competitive success and making public information that the public itself has underwritten. It could do no harm to release a more of that vast store of information and thereby contribute to a more informed public debate about the BBC's role.

At a structural level, beyond the release of research data, there is also need for a more formal level of accountability and participation. Despite the unique cash-based relationship between Corporation and viewers and listeners, there is little real perception that the BBC "belongs to us" – a sense of alienation that is not enhanced by the tabloid fashion for BBC-bashing. A greater sense of shared interest, of a genuinely community-based institution, would help to foster a healthy distrust for ideological or proprietorial vitriol against the BBC itself or its funding mechanism. We need to find some means, through elected representatives or external representative bodies, of initiating a dialogue between the BBC and its public. It would not just be good PR in the face of an increasingly bureaucratic and monolithic image. It would be good democracy.

Media titles available from John Libbey

ACAMEDIA RESEARCH MONOGRAPHS

Satellite Television in Western Europe
Richard Collins
Hardback ISBN 0 86196 203 6

Beyond the Berne Convention
Copyright, Broadcasting and the Single European Market
Vincent Porter
Hardback ISBN 0 86196 267 2

The Media Dilemma: Freedom and Choice or Concentrated Power?
Gareth Locksley
Hardback ISBN 0 86196 230 3

Nuclear Reactions: A Study in Public Issue Television
John Corner, Kay Richardson and Natalie Fenton
Hardback ISBN 0 86196 251 6

Transnationalization of Television in Western Europe
Preben Sepstrup
Hardback ISBN 0 86196 280 X

The People's Voice: Local Television and Radio in Europe
Nick Jankowski, Ole Prehn and James Stappers
Hardback ISBN 0 86196 322 9

BBC ANNUAL REVIEWS

Annual Review of BBC Broadcasting Research: No XV - 1989
Peter Menneer (ed)
Paperback ISBN 0 86196 209 5

Annual Review of BBC Broadcasting Research: No XVI - 1990
Peter Menneer (ed)
Paperback ISBN 0 86196 265 6

Published in association with UNESCO

Video World-Wide: An International Study
Manuel Alvarado (ed)
Paperback ISBN 0 86196 143 9

Media titles available from John Libbey

BROADCASTING STANDARDS COUNCIL PUBLICATIONS

A Measure of Uncertainty: The Effects of the Mass Media
Guy Cumberbatch and Dennis Howitt
Foreword by Lord Rees-Mogg
Hardback ISBN 0 86196 231 1

Violence in Television Fiction: Public Opinion and Broadcasting Standards
David Docherty
Paperback ISBN 0 86196 284 2

Survivors and the Media
Ann Shearer
Paperback ISBN 0 86196 332 6

Taste and Decency in Broadcasting
Andrea Millwood Hargrave
Paperback ISBN 0 86196 331 8

BROADCASTING RESEARCH UNIT MONOGRAPHS

Quality in Television – Programmes, Programme-makers, Systems
Richard Hoggart (ed)
Paperback ISBN 0 86196 237 0

Keeping Faith? Channel Four and its Audience
David Docherty, David E. Morrison and Michael Tracey
Paperback ISBN 0 86196 158 7

Invisible Citizens: British Public Opinion and the Future of Broadcasting
David E. Morrison
Paperback ISBN 0 86196 111 0

School Television in Use
Diana Moses and Paul Croll
Paperback ISBN 0 86196 308 3

Media titles available from John Libbey

Published in association with
THE ARTS COUNCIL of GREAT BRITAIN

Picture This: Media Representations of Visual Art and Artists
Philip Hayward (ed)
Paperback ISBN 0 86196 126 9

Culture, Technology and Creativity
Philip Hayward (ed)
Paperback ISBN 0 86196 266 4

ITC TELEVISION RESEARCH MONOGRAPHS

Television in Schools
Robin Moss, Christopher Jones and Barrie Gunter
Hardback ISBN 0 86196 314 8

IBA TELEVISION RESEARCH MONOGRAPHS

Teachers and Television:
A History of the IBA's Educational Fellowship Scheme
Josephine Langham
Hardback ISBN 0 86196 264 8

Godwatching: Viewers, Religion and Television
Michael Svennevig, Ian Haldane, Sharon Spiers and Barrie Gunter
Hardback ISBN 0 86196 198 6 Paperback ISBN 0 86196 199 4

Violence on Television: What the Viewers Think
Barrie Gunter and Mallory Wober
Hardback ISBN 0 86196 171 4 Paperback ISBN 0 86196 172 2

Home Video and the Changing Nature of Television Audience
Mark Levy and Barrie Gunter
Hardback ISBN 0 86196 175 7 Paperback ISBN 0 86196 188 9

Patterns of Teletext Use in the UK
Bradley S. Greenberg and Carolyn A. Lin
Hardback ISBN 0 86196 174 9 Paperback ISBN 0 86196 187 0

Attitudes to Broadcasting Over the Years
Barrie Gunter and Michael Svennevig
Hardback ISBN 0 86196 173 0 Paperback ISBN 0 86196 184 6

Media titles available from John Libbey

Television and Sex Role Stereotyping
Barrie Gunter
Hardback ISBN 0 86196 095 5 Paperback ISBN 0 86196 098 X

Television and the Fear of Crime
Barrie Gunter
Hardback ISBN 0 86196 118 8 Paperback ISBN 0 86196 119 6

Behind and in Front of the Screen - Television's Involvement with Family Life
Barrie Gunter and Michael Svennevig
Hardback ISBN 0 86196 123 4 Paperback ISBN 0 86196 124 2

UNIVERSITY OF MANCHESTER BROADCASTING SYMPOSIUM

And Now for the BBC ...
Proceedings of the 22nd Symposium 1991
Nod Miller and Rod Allen (eds)
Paperback ISBN 0 86196 318 0